C000153256

A 1950s
PORTSMOUTH
CHILDHOOD

VALERIE REILLY

The
History
Press

In loving memory of my mother,
Violet Urry, née Macklin (1917–84),
and my father, Frederick Urry (1902–76).

First published 2014

The History Press
The Mill, Brimscombe Port
Stroud, Gloucestershire, GL5 2QG
www.thehistorypress.co.uk

© Valerie Reilly, 2014

The right of Valerie Reilly to be identified as the
Author of this work has been asserted in accordance with the
Copyrights, Designs and Patents Act 1988.

All rights reserved. No part of this book may be reprinted
or reproduced or utilised in any form or by any electronic,
mechanical or other means, now known or hereafter invented,
including photocopying and recording, or in any information
storage or retrieval system, without the permission in writing
from the Publishers.

British Library Cataloguing in Publication Data.
A catalogue record for this book is available from the British Library.

ISBN 978 0 7509 5440 2

Typesetting and origination by The History Press
Printed in Great Britain

CONTENTS

ACKNOWLEDGEMENTS

I would like to thank all those people who have helped to put this book together and kindly allowed me to use their photographs and images.

Special thanks must go to my dear friend Margaret and her husband Tony Thomas, my cousins, Diane Williams, Jean Palmer and her brother John Organ and also friends Doreen and Ken Matthews, for all their interesting memories and photos.

I am grateful to Mark Walden, editor of *The News*, Portsmouth, for giving me permission to use some of the images from my 1980s *Yesterday* magazines.

Every effort was made to track down the owners of the images. If any mistakes have been made, I will endeavour to rectify them in any future publications.

ACKNOWLEDGMENTS

INTRODUCTION

Growing up in Portsmouth in the 1950s, into a family of small-time entertainers meant that my childhood was noisy but fun. Housing and money was short so soon after the Second World War, so our house was always full of relations and lodgers.

There wasn't any money left for holidays, but this didn't matter in Portsmouth. It was just a short bus ride or walk to Southsea beach – with a pack of sandwiches and a flask of tea – and the day at the seaside was free. There were several cinemas, theatres and local shops to visit and parks to play in. The family lived close by and we all celebrated Christmas, birthday teas and firework parties together then. All this, together with memories of schooldays, friends and the games we played in the street and at home made the '50s in Portsmouth very special to me.

For me, being a Pompey child – born in 1946 and growing up in the 1950s – brings back many memories of happy, carefree days. Portsmouth was heavily bombed during the Second World War and there were still bombsites and large craters to remind everyone how lucky they were to have survived it all. This must have made people appreciate the little things in life, as nobody in my family seemed to complain about not having this and that, as we all made do then. It was a case of 'if it works, then use it, if it breaks, then mend it and if it's beyond repair, then make it into something else'.

My father was very good at repairing anything, either with a lick of paint or a few screws or nails, glue or an extra piece of wood. He removed screws and hinges and nails from any furniture that was broken and then used the wood to make something else. All buttons were cut off badly worn clothing to be reused and the clothing was then used for cleaning rags. Old woollens were unpicked and knitted into something else; maybe a scarf, gloves or a hat. Nothing was wasted in the 1950s, especially leftover food, which would always be used to make another meal. Not having a fridge or freezer meant shopping for fresh food had to be a daily occurrence.

With very few cars about, most Portsmouth residents lived and worked in the same area and the main employer was the Portsmouth Dockyard. In fact, most families had several members working there. This all helped to keep the local shops, pubs and entertainment venues busy and profitable.

The dockyard in Portsmouth has been in existence for 500 years and remains one of the country's greatest assets, of great importance to the Royal Navy. The yard, as most Portsmouth residents called it, was a major employer in the 1950s. Many civilians were employed as young apprentices in various trades; as skilled and unskilled labourers, ship builders and clerical staff. Most of the workers were known as Dockies. In 1963, there were about 12,000 employed by the dockyard, but unfortunately this has gradually declined over the years. By 1981, for example, this number had been reduced, due to redundancies and retirement, to 7,500. Since then, several redundancies have been announced and in 2013 it was suggested that shipbuilding will cease and most of the dockyard could be closed by 2015.

Portsmouth was once known as a city of great military and naval importance, but the main focus now seems to be on tourism and leisure.

Family ties were of utmost importance in Portsmouth then, so there weren't many elderly people left on their own. Most families lived in the same street, or at least the same area, and could visit often. It wasn't unusual for Granny or Granddad to live with a son or daughter – or vice versa – and this helped

Me on a trike in my grandma Macklin's garden in Twyford Avenue, 1949.

with the family finances. This also meant the children always had a babysitter if Mum and Dad wanted a night out. Clothes, equipment and toys were handed down from one child to the next and then passed to a close relation or friend with children. You would most probably have an aunt or grandmother who was always ready with a batch of homemade cakes or pickles. It was very much an era where we helped one another without expecting payment: 'you scratch my back, and I'll scratch yours.' There was a real community spirit among the people of Portsmouth in the 1950s.

Most mothers stayed home for the first few years of a child's life, so there was the stability of having someone who loved and cared for you. Besides, nurseries would have been too expensive for most people. If a mother needed to work, then there was usually someone living close by to look after the children.

It was safe for children to play out in the street as very few cars came down the side roads. The children in each road would play ball, chasing and racing games. They could form a circle in the middle of the road and play games such as 'The Farmer Wants a Wife', or 'Ring a Ring o' Roses'. There was space to ride a bike, scooter or a pair of roller skates without getting in the way of a neighbour. Older children were allowed to go to the local park – with a warning from Mum to not talk to strangers – and were quite safe from harm, so long as they adhered to her words. Unless the weather was really bad, we children of the '50s never wanted to play indoors and were all more than happy to play in the street or even in our own garden if we had one. We didn't need or want expensive toys; with a bit of imagination, we could play at being anything we liked. You could be a cowboy with just a piece of wood as a rifle or your fingers as a pistol, hiding behind bushes or a pile of sand in the road, away from your enemy. There were also various skipping games which could be played with a length of your mother's washing line, if you didn't have a proper skipping rope.

Not many people had a television in the early 1950s, and if you did, it was only on for a few hours, as we all had various hobbies to occupy us on dark evenings at home. Most women made or mended their own clothes and some knitted or did some other craft. The men enjoyed gardening, and most gardens had a vegetable plot, no matter how small. Some men – my own father included – were proficient at woodwork and able to make small toys or furniture. Dad also mended the family's shoes. Instead of going to the hairdressers, mums learnt to cut their children's hair, and sometimes their own, too. Board games were often played with the whole family joining in, or a jigsaw would be shared and left on a board at the end of the table. We listened to music on a record player, or programmes on the radio and read books, magazines and comics. Telephones were not in many homes then either, so we wrote letters to family and friends who lived further away.

The pavements in Portsmouth seemed to be much cleaner then. We didn't have many takeaways in Portsmouth – except fish and chips, of course – so the streets weren't awash with cartons and burger wrappers. I suppose with so few cars, there was also very little pollution. That was until the winter, when the coal fires sent out clouds of smoke through the chimneys, creating a fog. Without the traffic we have today, the streets were much quieter, as well. In fact, it could be rather tranquil at times, which was less stressful when out for a walk with a friend, as you could hear each other speak.

There were very few supermarkets in Portsmouth, and they were only small, anyway. Most of the shops had someone behind a counter to serve you and give you advice on their product. This meant that anyone living on their own could have a little chat with somebody every day, even if it was only the butcher or the baker. Most goods were loose and not packaged, so you bought what you required without waste and there was no packaging to fill up the dustbin. Moreover, the shops didn't have piped music to drive you crazy whilst you browsed the shelves, which meant you could concentrate on the things you required.

Housing was in short supply in Portsmouth so soon after the war, with many houses bombed or destroyed, so relations shared their homes with others until they were rehoused. Newly married couples usually had a room in the bride or groom's parents' house until they could afford to rent or buy one of their own. My parents' house was full to overflowing at times with relations and lodgers, but we managed somehow and there was always somebody to talk to or share a problem with. The lovely little prefabricated houses that were put together quickly after the war did solve a few housing problems, though: these were built in Paulsgrove and on top of Portsdown Hill. They were quite cosy and served a purpose until the housing estates were finished in Paulsgrove and Leigh Park, where several Portsmouth families eventually went to live.

We must have all been a great deal healthier in the 1950s, as we walked more. Without a car waiting outside the front door ready to take us a few yards up the road, we didn't become lazy. Even if we needed to catch a bus, we had to walk to the bus stop. In Portsmouth most things were just

Prefabs being built on Portsdown Hill. (*Yesterday Magazine*)

a short walk away; we had cinemas, theatres, shops, pubs, schools, hospitals and parks, all in the locality. So long as you were fairly agile, you could walk to Southsea beach or Clarence Pier, both of which had all the amenities for a good day out, especially in the summer. It was rare for people to be able to afford a holiday abroad or even a week in a boarding house or hotel, so being close to the beach and countryside made Portsmouth a great place to live. There were several coach trips available in the summer months to various places and these were quite reasonably priced, so we never felt we were missing out by not having a holiday away.

Life seemed so much simpler in the 1950s: there was less money, and not so much choice in food and material things, but we were easier to please because of this. We may only remember the good times and the sunny days, but I loved life as a child in that era.

one

HOUSE
AND HOME

'That's not a baby, it's a blooming elephant,' laughed my parents' good friend Fred Flewin when he came to see me in St Mary's Hospital, Portsmouth, where I was born in November 1946. Fred and his wife Doris ran a greengrocer's shop in Fratton Road, Portsmouth, called Flewins, and Mum told me that they bought some lovely things for me as a baby. I was born by caesarean section, as mum was so tiny and I was quite large. In those days, it was such a serious procedure that she had to stay in hospital for two weeks to recover. As I was born before the NHS was in operation, my parents had to pay £25 for my arrival; that must have been a lot of money to find in those days.

Between 1940 and 1945, Mum had worked at Airspeed in Portsmouth, making the wings of aircraft. She loved that job and was good at it; she was even commended by the Lord Mayor for her good work. Of course, when the war was over, the men came back and had to have their jobs back. My mother was very disappointed and had to take a

Fred and Doris Flewin, owners of Flewins greengrocer's in the 1950s.

job cleaning carriages at Southern Trains at Fratton until November 1946, when I was born. At the time, my father used the train to travel from his sister Alice Newman's house and antique shop in Fishbourne, where he was living at the time, to Portsmouth Dockyard where he worked. He used to chat to Mum when he got off the train, and they became friendly. This must have been in September 1945.

Violet Macklin with workmates at Southern Railways, Fratton Station, around 1945.

The next time they met was in the Royal Dragoon pub in Kingston Crescent, Portsmouth. My father's friend George Martin was landlord of the pub and Dad sometimes played the drums there to accompany the pianist. My mother came into the Royal Dragoon with some friends one evening in 1945 and started messing about on the piano, with my father playing the drums. Soon after that my parents started courting and became engaged, and then married on 29 December the same year. They had to marry in Portsmouth register office as Dad had been married years ago and was now divorced. (Once sited in St Michael's Road, it has now been relocated to Milldam House in Burnaby Road. The old building is now a pub named the Registry.) The Church then refused to marry them and because of that Mum wouldn't have me christened after I was born. She always said that as she wasn't good enough for the Church, then the Church wasn't good enough for her daughter, so I remained a heathen.

The Royal Dragoon pub closed down in 1970 to make way for the Baltic Office block, one of many pub closures since the 1950s.

When Mum and I left hospital after two weeks' confinement, I started my life in Portsmouth at No.45 Twyford Avenue in Stamshaw. It was then the home of my grandparents, May and Harry Macklin. The front of the house was used as a shop, where Gran sold second-hand furniture, clothes and toys; in fact, anything of value. Most of the stock was bought or given to her by the wealthy ladies she visited in Southsea. The shop was quite dark and the flooring was bare boards. The stock was scattered around the shop, with clothing hung up on rails. At the back of the shop was Gran's living room, filled with heavy wooden Victorian furniture, including a large leather chaise longue, which had horsehair coming out of a split in the back of it. There was a dining table over by a window, and on top of it was a red chenille cover. Her kitchen was in a glass conservatory leading into the garden and I remember Gran boiling live lobsters in a large pot out there. I'm sure I heard them scream.

Gran's garden had long grass and very few flowers, so it was a bit wild looking. An enormous iron gasometer towered above the houses, way beyond her garden. This huge metal building in Rudmore was demolished in 1978, when Commercial Road was widened. In the corner of Gran's garden stood a huge pile of junk: old buckets, broken chairs and old furniture. This was probably from the shop, but it was still a bit of an eyesore. In the summer, Gran would sit in the garden on an old chair with a jug of stout, which had been purchased from the snug in the Air Balloon pub, opposite the house. She would have a glass in one hand and her cat Peedy for company, whilst I rode up and down on my trike. Gran was well known in this area of Portsmouth, as she gave some of the poorer families clothes for their children, as well as loaning money.

Grandma's favourite pub, the Air Balloon, was one of approximately 1,000 pubs in Portsmouth years ago; there was one on almost every street corner. Being a naval town, they were all very busy then. Without television and the technology we have today, the pub was the main focus of entertainment, especially for men. There was usually a public bar where the working man or sailor could meet up for a drink, a smoke and game of cards, dominoes or darts. Some of the Portsmouth pubs were quite small; not much larger than the front room of a house. This was the case for many pubs when they started out.

Me and my grandmother, May Macklin, in the garden of Twyford Avenue in 1949.

The Air Balloon sadly closed in 2005 and was due to be turned into flats. An arson attack damaged the building in 2007, but it is now being renovated. There are now only about 100 pubs left in Portsmouth at present.

The site that Gran's shop occupied was eventually demolished to make way for the flyover built in the 1970s. Quite a few large and lovely old houses were destroyed in the name of progress in Portsmouth over the years, not necessarily due to being bombed. In the 1930s, Gran, Granddad and my mother Violet lived close by, in a grand old Georgian house at No.535 Commercial Road in Mile End.

It was three storeys high with a basement as well as a large ballroom, in which my mum used to teach tap dancing; she would put on shows for charity and in hospitals during the war. I think a Mavis Butler ran a dance school from there in the 1950s. The house was painted black and white, and before Gran took over the lease, it was known as Doctor Blackman's house. The house used to be a listed building, but caught fire, which was very convenient as the space was needed for the flyover.

OUR FIRST MOVE

When I was a few months old, my parents and I moved to a house in Arthur Street, near Kingston Crescent, Portsmouth. It was a two-up two-down flat-fronted terrace, next to a pub. I don't remember the front room: I think maybe we had a lodger living in there. I do remember one lodger called Bill, though; I think he was the brother of a family friend. He had a mass of wild grey curly hair and sometimes he gave me sixpence, saying, 'Here you are, a tanner for a tiddler.' The back room was all dark wood, with canvas on the floor, a rag rug by the fire and dark, heavy furniture. There was a high mantelpiece with a large wireless standing on the top. Mum used to listen to *Mrs Dale's Diary*, *The Archers* and *Woman's Hour*, and we all loved *Dick Barton – Special Agent*.

At the back of this room was a small kitchen, or scullery, as Mum referred to it. There were no modern conveniences at all; just a grey and white iron stove and a large, square Butler sink. All the washing of clothes, dishes and bodies was done in this sink, including me as a baby. I remember my lovely Dad using it for his evening wet shave, with a striped towel around

Me in my pram in Arthur Street, 1947.

his neck. I watched him in fascination whilst he lathered his chin and upper lip with soap from a thick cup and a small bristle brush. He then sliced it off with his razor that had been sharpened on a leather strop hanging on the wall.

We didn't have a bathroom in this house so, once a week, the large galvanised bath was brought into the living room and all the family could have a good soak. This would be in front of the fire if it was winter.

From left to right: my grandfather Harry Macklin, Joyce, me in Jessie's arms, Iris Delves and my parents, Violet and Fred Urry.

Outside was a cobblestone yard, with high brick walls surrounding it. This is also where the toilet was. It had a wooden seat and a high cistern with a chain pull, with Izal medicated toilet paper that scratched your bottom when you used it. There was just enough room for me to play with my doll's pram out in the yard, and I used to push it up and down with the cat in it.

I was able to ride my three-wheeled Triang tricycle up and down the pavement, at the front of the house in Arthur Street. There were no cars in our street and all the neighbours would watch over other people's children. One day, when I was about 3 years old, a man asked me to sit on the windowsill while he took my photograph. I was scared stiff and didn't relax, even when Mum said it was okay. This resulted in a very sulky looking photo of me in the family album.

As I was so young, the only other memory of this address was an off-licence in Kingston Crescent. In the window sat a moving male mannequin, with a glass in one hand and a bottle of stout in the other (maybe it was Mackeson). The poor chap spent his time pouring out his drink but not getting to taste it.

MOVING AGAIN

My parents were unusual in being able to purchase their own house. In about 1950, my parents were able to buy a house – No.6 Beresford Road, North End, Portsmouth – with the aid of a mortgage. The house had three bedrooms, two reception rooms, a kitchen and an upstairs bathroom, and it was a bay and forecourt building. Dad was clever at making things, so soon had the house looking good. It was a bright and fresh-looking place, so different to Arthur Street, and I loved it. There was plenty of space for us and it had a lovely little garden too.

Housing and money was in short supply in those early years after the war. The house cost £1,600, which was a lot of money for my parents in those days. It was very unusual for a working-class couple to be able to buy their own property in 1950, so they must have saved a fair deposit.

SHARING THE HOME

Three of my grandparents came from a long line of Portsmouth families: the Clarks, the Urrys and the Marshes. Among their many trades and professions were fishermen, publicans, shoemakers, cork cutters, sailors and shipwrights.

Grandma Macklin, née Clark, was ill for quite a while and had to spend a long time in hospital. By the time she was better, her little shop in Twyford Avenue had been rented to someone else and Granddad was living with his sister back in London, so my father built him a room under the stairs for when he came to stay. This was just large enough for a single bed. Dad fixed a light on the wall and Granddad kept his clothes in a suitcase under his bed. Gran came to live with us in Beresford Road and she took up residence in our front room until she died in 1956. Gran was diagnosed with diabetes and every day a district nurse came to give her an injection in her leg. We had some of her old furniture in that room, including a large black mirrored cabinet along one wall with all her china and glass displayed on the shelves, along with a beautiful green glass tea set. She had a single bed, a dining table and chairs, plus an armchair next to the fireplace. Gran would sit so close to the coal fire in winter that her legs were red and mottled.

My grandmother always liked to look the part, even when she was very ill; the nurses all called her 'the Duchess'.

Whenever Gran went out, she wore a fur coat and a large hat with wax fruit or flowers on the top. I had to put metal curlers in her hair to give it a curl and then she would put on her jewellery, which she kept in a small square wooden box. Every evening, Gran would go over to the Pelham pub on the corner of Chichester Road for a bottle of stout.

My grandmother May Macklin in her fur coat, with me and my cousin Diane LeMettey at Milton Locks in 1952.

Gran was brought up in the Rudmore Cellars Pub in Portsmouth, as her parents George and May Clark were the tenants somewhere between 1900 and the 1920s. Most of her family still lived in Rudmore in the 1950s. The Rudmore Cellars was sadly demolished in 2009, and the ferry port now stands on the site. Most of the pubs in Portsmouth were owned by the Brickwoods Brewery, which was sited near the dockyard from 1848 until 1971. It was then taken over by Whitbread. The building was demolished in 1989 and the site is now used as a car park.

My grandfather, Henry Warner Macklin, was born in Lambeth in London in 1880. His father Thomas had a hansom cab business, and was once a groom in a large house. Granddad ran away to sea when he was 14 years old and lied about his age to get into the Royal Navy. He met my grandmother when he was stationed in Portsmouth in 1902 and stayed in

The Rudmore Cellars, run by my great-grandparents Mary and George Clark in around 1910.

the city. Granddad ran a fruit and veg business in Southsea in the '50s. I spent some time with him one day and enquired why the front of the stall showed lovely fresh fruit but he served customers the bruised produce from the back. I wasn't invited there again. Granddad wore grey woollen trousers with braces over a striped shirt with replaceable white stiff collars. On his waistcoat he had a fob watch on a chain and he wore a large cap to keep his balding head warm. His glasses were round and wire-rimmed and he smoked Player's Navy Cut cigarettes.

When Granddad became ill on one of his visits I had to give up my room, as we couldn't expect the doctor to tend him under the stairs. Granddad died in that room, so I didn't want to sleep in there for a long time afterwards.

I never met my paternal grandparents, Charles and Ann Urry, as they both died in 1943, before I was born. They were both born in Portsmouth and for several years lived in Highgate Road in Copnor, close to other members of the Urry clan. My grandfather was a corkcutter and he made corks for beer, wine, medicine bottles and beer barrels. Granddad delivered the corks to various businesses in Portsmouth, such as Brickwoods Brewery and Timothy Whites, the chemist. There was a selection of cork pictures that he made, displayed in the Connaught Drill Hall near the Portsmouth Guildhall. He was well known in Portsmouth, as 'Corky'.

For families in the 1950s, it was a constant struggle to make ends meet. My family found several ways to help pay the bills, though.

The wages were quite low; I think the average man's wage in the 1950s was less than £10 in Portsmouth. Working women earned much less than men, even if they did the same job. Dad always did overtime and night work, which paid more money. My mum took in lodgers and sometimes did a cleaning job if funds were short. As my father was a drummer and Mum played the piano, they would earn extra cash entertaining in pubs, clubs and at functions at weekends. My parents didn't use a bank as there was no money left over for savings; every last penny was used to pay bills, or put towards food and clothing. Mum had a long green metal box with slots along the top, and into each section she put money towards the mortgage, food and household expenses, which included the gas and electricity meters. They were situated under the stairs, and Mum fed the meters with enough 1s pieces to last each day. If the electric ever ran out in the evening, there would be a mad dash to refill it in the dark, with help from a torch or a candle. We didn't have the expense of a phone or car, and holidays abroad were out of the question for us then. Workers were paid in cash each week, and sometimes if Mum's purse was empty by the end of the week, she would meet my father at the dockyard gates so they could both go shopping together for food for the weekend.

The rooms in the house my parents bought were soon filled to help with the finances. My parents let out the bedrooms upstairs to lodgers to help pay the bills. As a result, Mum and Dad had to sleep in the sitting room on a three-seater red patterned sofa that folded out into a bed. Mum called it a bed settee, and it was very comfortable, as long as you didn't sit at the back, as it would close up on you. Next to the sofa was a single bed that folded into a table; this often became my bed while I was small. There was a time when every room in the house, except the kitchen and bathroom, was used as a bedroom for either a relative or lodger.

When times were difficult, we had two male lodgers sharing the large bedroom. The other bedroom was quite small, and sometimes we would have a single lodger staying in there. Mum was a very generous landlady and served up huge meals, as well as a pile of sandwiches for the lodgers to take for lunch at work. She did their laundry and cleaned their room. It was no wonder then that one man, a Mr Snowball, returned again and again. Mum often became fed up having strangers to look after and sometimes pretended that she was selling the house, so they had to go. A few months later, when she was short of cash, she advertised the room again and back would come Mr Snowball. There was never a shortage of male lodgers in 1950s Portsmouth; I expect this was due to the aftermath of the war.

For a year or so in 1957, Mum became a bit too ambitious, with regard to lodgers. She also wished for us to have a house to ourselves, so she filled No.6 Beresford Road with lodgers and rented No.9 for us to live in. This was fine for a while, but Mum should have hired an accountant as her outgoings outstripped the income received from the lodgers. Soon that idea failed and we moved back into our own house.

For a while, I slept in the little middle bedroom, on a single iron bedstead with a blue and white bedspread on top. On my bedside table stood a Cinderella alarm clock and a blue plastic children's lamp. There was a small pearl-white dancing lady on the front and when you wound her up, she played the Brahms lullaby. The fire in that room wasn't lit unless I was ill, so it was rather cold in the winter. I liked the cold bedroom, though, as the air was always fresh and clear; not stuffy, like centrally heated homes are now. Also, everyone smoked in those days, so the rooms downstairs smelt of stale smoke. My bed was warm and cosy with several blankets and flannelette sheets, plus a rubber hot-water bottle put into my bed by Mum before bedtime. There was only a small rug next to my bed and canvas under that, so you had to hop from one rug to the next to prevent cold feet.

I have vivid memories of one lodger in particular: a lady called Emily Hedger, who lived in the end bedroom of the house for many years. A friend of my mum's, she used to lodge in Gran's house, so when Gran had to give up the shop, Emily came to live with us. She took up residence in the end bedroom, along with all her belongings. There was a large iron bedstead in the middle of the room, and on one side stood a heavy dressing table covered with silver-framed pictures of her family, plus other treasures. A huge chest of drawers stood on the other side of the bed, with a bottom drawer full of sheets, towels and linen. Emily was born in the late 1800s and the First World War must have robbed her of the chance to marry, as most of the linen was still in wrappers. She was also a bit of a hoarder and had tins and boxes full of sweets, matches and bars of soap. Clothes and shoes dating back to the 1920s were still in her wardrobe, never to be worn again, and I remember the room smelling strongly of mothballs.

Emily only paid a small rent for her room and enjoyed living within the family unit, sharing meals and leisure time in the evenings. In exchange for this, she babysat me and helped with all the household chores, mainly doing the jobs that Mum didn't like. Emily was always up early (after Dad, who left home to walk to work in the dockyard at about 6 a.m.). In the winter, Emily always cleaned out the grate and laid a fire with paper, wooden sticks and coal, to make a blazing fire for when Mum and I got up. When I was very young and it was cold, she used to put a bowl of warm water in front of the fire for my wash in the morning, with a separate tumbler of warm water for cleaning my teeth. Emily did the washing up, cleaned the kitchen and kept her own room spotless. She used to sit on the outside of her bedroom windowsill, cleaning the panes every week.

Emily worked for years in Smith's crisp factory, based in Mile End, Portsmouth, painting the inside of the large tins blue. The tins were then filled with small bags of crisps before they were delivered to the shops and pubs. She told me that one day, whilst about to paint the inside of a tin, she found a large rat inside and he sunk his teeth into her hand and refused to let go. One of her male colleagues had to prise open the rat's mouth to release her.

The Smith's crisp factory was moved out of Mile End, Portsmouth and into Paulsgrove in 1953. The company was taken over by PepsiCo in the 1990s, but some of the products from Smiths are still available under the Walkers name.

Emily's uniform consisted of a green wraparound overall, with matching cap. At home she wore a similar outfit, but with a floral or paisley pattern on it. She only dressed up when she was visiting her family or did her annual shopping trip, when she would buy all her Christmas and birthday cards and presents, plus any clothes she needed to replace. Emily then wore a very smart burgundy dress and black tie-up shoes. Her coat was the same colour and she wore a pretty silk scarf, but always spoilt the effect by placing a beret underneath it. She put a large padlock on her bedroom door to prevent anyone nosing in her room, as she always did whenever she went out. Emily was kind and caring and always bought me a large doll for Christmas (and jewellery for Mum), but she was also very frugal. She had her own hairdressing scissors

Emily Hedger, in her overall, and me outside my dad's shed in Beresford Road, 1954.

and Mum cut her hair whenever she needed it. Emily sat on a wooden chair in the middle of the room and Mum just cut around her hair in a straight line. She wore it straight with a parting on one side and no fringe.

In the evening, after the washing up was done, Emily always sat close by the fire, smoothing a green, foul-smelling piece of Snowfire into her hands. This, she said, was to prevent chilblains. Curled up on her lap was our old tabby cat, Buster. I sat close to her and she taught me nursery rhymes and children's stories such as 'Red Riding Hood', 'Goldilocks and the Three Bears'

Emily – in her best frock – with me in 1951.

and 'The Three Pigs'. She often fell asleep in that chair and it was only the fireguard that prevented an accident occurring. At Christmas, Emily always went back home to her sister Ethel and family, who lived in a large house in Mile End, close to Charles Dickens' birthplace.

SANCTUARY IN THE GARDEN

In a house bustling with people, I would often escape into the garden. The toilet was just outside the back door and was a toilet pan with a wooden seat that Dad had carved himself. There was a large iron cistern tank above the toilet, with a long metal chain to pull and flush. We had Izal toilet paper which was hard on your bottom, but it was still a better choice than the pieces of newspaper hung on a string to use if the Izal ran out. With all the people living in our house, the toilet was the only place to go for peace and quiet. I used to sit out there and read the extra papers out loud, pretending I was the newsreader on the radio, sing songs at the top of my voice and talk to my imaginary friends. The neighbours must have thought I was bonkers.

My favourite place of all was the garden, which seemed huge when I was young but was really quite tiny. A door led from the living room into the garden, down a high stone step onto a small patio area. In the summer I sat on this step, shelling peas from their pods into a bowl. They were so crisp and sweet that several of them would always disappear into my mouth. The patio was just large enough for me to play games with my dolls. If I played what I called mummies and daddies (although the daddy was invisible), the stone step became a sofa for my dolls to sit on. My father was a good amateur carpenter and could turn any old piece of wood he found into a toy or piece of furniture. Over the years he made me a cot, cooker, dresser and a small table and chairs for my dolls.

I had several dolls, most of them bought for me at Christmas. Being an only child, these became my friends when I was alone in the garden. They were my pupils in school with the wooden desk and blackboard, also made by Dad. On another day, they became patients in hospital, with me as their nurse. Mum even made me a nurse's outfit out of an old sheet with a red cross painted on the front. I had a plastic doctor's set to check on their heartbeats and temperature,

Me with toys made by my father in the garden of Beresford Road in 1952.

with another piece of sheet cut up into bandages. Sometimes, Mum brought some chairs outside and my dolls were placed on these so I could pretend it was a bus. I loved the bus conductor set I had, especially the clipper for the tickets.

There was a pathway going round the garden in an H shape with flowers in the border on either side. Just past the small patio was a patch of grass, and when it was hot, Mum made a tent from an old blanket across this area, tying the corners to the fence with string. With some old mats inside, I could continue my games in the cool. On occasion, I was allowed to have a meal in there, especially if my best friend Margaret

Me in my nurse's outfit, made by my mother, in 1952.

or my cousin Diane came to play. Dad also built a large swing for me, stretching across the pathway. It was made of heavy, thick wood with a wooden seat and sisal rope, which made your hands sting a bit after a while. I loved to swing up high, peeking over the fence at all our neighbours, busy in their gardens. If I lay right back, I could imagine another world going on in the clouds above me.

Mum turned the other area in front of the grass into her vegetable plot. Here she grew tomatoes, lettuce, radishes, potatoes and spring onions. She tied silver foil from her cigarette packet and milk bottle tops onto string to scare the birds away, which I liked because it made a soft tinkling noise when it was quiet in the garden. Her runner beans grew up the strings attached to the trellis on the wall that separated our garden from the neighbours'.

DAD'S SHED

At the end of the garden was Dad's special place: his shed. It had a brick-built base, windows around the top and an iron corrugated roof. It was in here that Dad made my toys and small pieces of furniture like coffee tables, although he did once make a cocktail cabinet out of a tea chest and pieces of wood that he found. It was about 4ft tall and 2ft wide, with a cupboard at the bottom for bottles and large glasses. At the top was a door that opened widthways with mirrors at the back, and he fitted metal cocktail sticks and a chrome lemon squeezer onto these. We had tiny decorated glasses with gold rims standing on a glass tray in here. He was so proud of his work that he showed everyone that came to the house.

Inside his shed were two iron feet that he used to put shoes on for mending, one smaller than the other. There were pieces of leather to cut out for the soles and small drawers full of nails and screws, some of which had been removed from old furniture. The shed was like Aladdin's cave: full of wood, old tins of paint, brushes of every size and type. Saws, chisels and all sizes of hammer and screwdriver all fought for space along the wall and bench, which also had large and small iron vices for holding wood in place whilst Dad shaved it with his large wooden plane. The floor beneath his feet was deep with sawdust and wood shavings, which never got swept up. I thought that one day my father would be buried in it. On the windowsill was a metal pot with hard glue inside it. When Dad needed to use this to stick anything, he put it onto the gas hob to melt and it smelt revolting.

DOMESTIC CHORES

I clearly remember the difficulty in keeping a clean house in 1950s Portsmouth. We didn't have any mod cons for cleaning (like a vacuum cleaner for example), but it didn't matter, as there weren't any carpets on the floor, only rugs. Mum and Emily took all the mats into the garden and hung them on the line for a good beating with a broom. They then swept and mopped all through the house from one end to the other, and upstairs too. The furniture would then be smothered with wax polish from a tin of Mansion House. Then, once it was dry, it would all be buffed to a shine with a duster. The next job was the silver, which was cleaned by pushing it into the earth in the garden and polishing it till it shone. Mum used Brasso for cleaning the brass letterbox and any ornaments we had made of brass or copper. Dad also used this for polishing his cymbals for his drum set. I remember the windows having a lovely shine, due to being polished with vinegar in water and rubbed with newspaper.

Mum and Granddad were both heavy smokers; Mum smoked Craven 'A' cork-tipped cigarettes, while Granddad preferred Senior Service cigarettes. Dad was a social smoker, so only had a few of Mum's each day. Because of this, the paintwork and wallpaper downstairs was quite yellow with nicotine by the time spring came. Every year, therefore, Dad redecorated those rooms. The wallpaper was usually white with bold bright flowers, and the wood was painted cream. The walls outside, facing the garden, were painted green and brown and the front of the house was cream with a varnished front door. Dad used to brush a pattern on the varnish with a stiff brush while the varnish was wet, which he called graining. If there was a mark on the wallpaper, it could be removed by rubbing it with a piece of bread. Dad would then clean paint off his hands with white spirit, and rub them with baby oil and sugar to make them soft again.

In the corner of our kitchen, by the window, was a large Butler sink. Underneath this was some shelving, where Mum kept the tin of Vim to clean the sink and the bath. There was also a box of Lux washing flakes and one of Tide detergent for clothes and a large bar of Sunlight soap for cleaning the floors, plus a bottle of Lifeguard disinfectant. Later in the '50s we had fairy liquid to wash up the dishes too. These were all hidden behind a cotton curtain hanging in the front.

I remember that when I was small, I was stood on a chair at the sink and allowed to wash up the cups with a small cotton mop. I sometimes stood there so long playing with the bubbles that my arms were red and raw and my fingers were white and wrinkled.

The grey and white iron oven stood against another wall, with all the aluminium saucepans resting on top of the eye-level grill. I believe these ovens were rented from the gas board, although I couldn't be sure about that. A very large kettle rested on the hob and it was always on the boil. This was needed to supply the countless cups of Typhoo tea made with leaves in a teapot, with a small strainer held over each cup to catch the leaves. We also had a bottle of Camp coffee essence, which my mother enjoyed on occasion. The kettle was a necessity to supply hot water for washing dishes, clothes, hands and faces, as we had no hot water tap or tank.

In a recess was a large gas copper to wash all the white cotton sheets etc. A long stick was used to agitate the clothes and this was white, thin and soft after many uses. The copper made our small kitchen so full of hot steam that it became unbearable and all the windows and doors had to be flung open, even in the winter. Eventually, Mum had it taken out and instead sent all the bed linen, tea towels and Dad's best shirts to Chapman's Laundry, based in Kingston Crescent in Portsmouth. The company sent a van round each week to collect the dirty linen; this was tied up in brown paper with a long tag listing the contents. In return, you received last week's laundry, all clean, starched and pressed. The site that Chapman's Laundry occupied is now the Sovereigns pub.

All the other clothes were washed by hand in the sink and put on the line in the garden to dry. Sometimes the clothes would be hanging on the long clothes line for a few days, if there was no wind to dry them. Large items – such as blankets, curtains and suchlike – were put into the bath, which was filled with hot soapy water and Mum would tread them in her bare feet, like you would grapes to make wine. How on earth she got them down the stairs and onto the line I will never know, but she did. She was a very strong woman, considering she was only 4ft 8in in height. When the washing was dry, Mum put a clean sheet on the dining table to do the ironing. We didn't own an electric iron, but instead had two small flat ones that Mum heated up on the hob or on the coal fire in winter. When she thought the iron was hot enough she spat on it; if it sizzled, then she ironed cotton first and delicate things once when the iron cooled down, using the other iron when it was hot enough. Mum always ironed everything – socks, towels and all our underwear – as well as the creased cotton clothes. She then put the clothes onto the wooden clothes horse to air in front of the fire in winter, or out in the fresh air on a warm day.

We had a long larder in the wall of the kitchen for all the other things, as we didn't own a fridge or freezer. Later on, Mum bought a large cabinet with cupboards at the bottom for tins and a drop-down breadbin. I remember that it also had an enamel worktop for making sandwiches and pastry. Above this was a sliding glass door with shelves for jars and biscuits, and the broom and cleaning things were stored in a cupboard on the side. This was blue and white, and quite modern at the time.

Later, Mum used to have a Provident cheque, supplied by a man she called 'the provy man'. She was then able to buy things with this cheque and pay him back weekly. The first item she bought was a small electric lightweight hoover in blue plastic, which made cleaning the floor much easier. Next, she bought a whole set of dinner plates and a tea service made of blue melamine. This set lasted for years, but it was difficult to get the tea stains off the cups. The Provident cheque could also be used in some shops for clothes and shoes.

—

The family home in Gloucester Street, Southsea, was bombed and we moved to Chesterfield Road in Copnor, Portsmouth, to live with my mum's parents, Charles and Edith Woods, and their cat Mickey. Granddad had an allotment at the back of the garden and I used to help him pull up the potatoes and pick the tomatoes. At the side of the allotments, there used to be old brickworks, where we kids used to play. There were also a lot of old metal Anderson shelters around there. In our garden at Chesterfield Road we had a brick-built air-raid shelter. There were no lights, so it was very dark and full of spiders. I also remember washing in a tin bath and the cat Mickey climbing up the chimney. Every day I used to wait at the window to see Granddad coming home from working in the dockyard.

Tony Thomas

We lived in a two-up two-down terrace house in Mayo Street, Portsmouth, when my brother John and I were children. There was no bathroom and the toilet was outside, with a small garden. The rooms were very small compared to the houses today. We only had an open fire in the living room which was also the dining room, and we listened to the radio in there.

Jean Palmer, née Organ

I lived in a terrace house with a forecourt in Balfour Road, Portsmouth. There was a long back garden with a swing. With hardly any cars in our road, we could play in the street safely. Front doors were left open. I shared a bedroom with my sister Linda and we had blackout curtains to shut out the sunlight in summer.

Doreen Matthews, née Linsdale

I lived in Newcome Road, Fratton, in Portsmouth. All the houses in the locality were terraced, and many of the housewives would sit on chairs by their front door knitting or chatting to passers-by. In the '50s, there were only one or two cars every 100 yards of street.

Ken Matthews

I was born in Wingfield Street, Stamshaw. The street was bombed during the war and we moved to Mayo Street, where my sister Jean was born. One end of this street was bombed and all the children at that end were killed. I remember all of us children playing on the bomb sites. Later we moved again into Havant Road, North End, where my paternal grandparents and Auntie Ethel lived. Our house was a flat-fronted terrace and we didn't have electricity to begin with, and only had gas mantles to give us light, with a coal fire for heating.

John Organ

[Margaret was born in Scotland in 1947, but her English sailor father brought the family to Portsmouth to live with his sister and family in the early 1950s.]

We lived at No.7 Balfour Road, Portsmouth, till I was about 8 years old. There was an upright piano in the front room and, as I didn't like the porridge, I poured it in the piano. When we moved to No.26 Balfour Road, there was an old coal shed in the garden which was cleaned out so I could play in it. There was also a large pear tree that I used to climb.

Margaret Thomas, née Gilkerson

Margaret Gilkerson with her mother, Ina, and her dog, Lucky, in Balfour Road, North End.

[Diane is the daughter of Roy and Joyce, who ran several pubs in the area. She remembers their first pub, the Shearer Arms.]

The Shearer Arms had a club room that was hired out for functions. One day, my parents did a wedding feast, and Dad and my uncle Harold laid out the tables with plates of sliced ham. Our dog managed to get into the room and gobbled up all the ham, leaving muddy footprints over the table and wedding cake. There was a frantic visit to the corner shop to get as much ham sliced by hand as we could. They covered up the marks on the cake with white chalk. I won't say what happened to the dog, no one ever knew! Ha!

Diane Williams, née LeMetty

KEEPING UP APPEARANCES

The Urry household in 1950s Portsmouth used fewer products than we do today.

Joyce and Roy LeMettey with their daughter, Diane. They were popular pub landlords in 1950s Portsmouth.

My father's name was Frederick William Urry, but he was always known as Jerry for reasons unknown to me. He worked in Portsmouth Dockyard as a skilled labourer in the Oxygen Plant from the 1940s until 1967. Dad enjoyed his working life, and worked part-time in Johnsons & Johnsons factory where they made the baby products, when he retired from the dockyard. The factory, in Cosham, was demolished to make way for an industrial estate.

My father was a smart and handsome man and, although he did a dirty job in the dockyard, still liked to look tidy. He wore his oldest suit – complete with waistcoat – to work and his shoes were always shiny. He had a hat for every occasion, and the trilby he wore to work was fluffed up over the steam of the kettle and brushed each morning. Whenever we went out visiting or socialising, he always looked the part. It had to be a smart three-piece suit, pristine white shirt with co-ordinating tie, false hanky on a piece of card in his top pocket and a flower in his buttonhole.

Dad was deaf in one ear due to a perforated eardrum, and so had to wear a cumbersome NHS hearing aid. There was a large plastic earpiece with a long wire leading to the battery holder which Dad tried to conceal in his waistcoat pocket under his suit coat; he really hated people knowing he was deaf. He used to be so embarrassed when the thing whistled loudly in public. Sometimes at family gatherings in one of Mum's relatives' homes, Dad became bored trying hard to listen to all the conversation and fell asleep in an armchair after switching the hearing aid off.

Hair was shampooed once a week in the kitchen sink with Vosene shampoo then towel dried in front of the fire in winter and out in the sunshine when it was warm.

The bathroom in our second house was upstairs; it was quite small, with a bath and a sink on a pedestal. There was no heating so, in the winter, Mum put a paraffin heater in there for our weekly bath. Above the bath was a large, noisy Ascot heater for hot water. This was a frightening piece of equipment that shook with effort whilst flames shot out of the gap and water came gushing out of the spout. In the bath we crumbled a Cussons scented bath cube and washed ourselves with a bar of Lux, Camay, Pears or Lifebuoy soap. At Christmas I sometimes received a bar of soap shaped like a cartoon character or soldier and I never wanted to use it. My toothpaste came in a round tin and it was a pink powder.

By that point, Dad shaved with a Gillette safety razor, but continued to use his bristle brush and shaving soap in a large thick cup. Brylcreem was smeared into his hair to comb it into shape with a slight quiff on the forehead. In the garden stood a large galvanised bath to catch the rainwater, and Dad used this to rinse his face and hair each day, then patted glycerine and Rosewater onto his face and hands. His skin was as soft as a baby's bottom. Dad had dentures, so cleaned them with Eucryl tooth powder from a tin.

My mother was a casual dresser, unless she was going somewhere special, in which case she wore a suit – or 'costume' as she called it – together with a pillbox hat. She only wore make-up (always Max Factor) for certain occasions: Crème Puff powder in a compact, blue eyeshadow and bright-red lipstick. The rouge she wore on her cheeks came in a tiny blue box by Bourgeois, who also made the perfume she wore – called 'Evening in Paris' – in a small blue bottle with a silver cap.

MEDICATION

In the 1950s, most people only went to the doctor if they were really ill, as the National Health Service only started in 1948; before that, you had to pay. Most houses had their own stock of medicines and solutions to common complaints, as well as the usual complement of rolls of bandages, gauze and sticking plasters on a roll.

Senna pods, soaked in boiling water, were drunk as a remedy for constipation for adults. As a child, I was given a spoonful of Syrup of Figs for the same thing. I was often given a spoonful of castor oil mixed with honey, to make it palatable. It seems that everyone was obsessed with bowel movements in those days. If you had an upset tummy due to overindulgence you could take a small glass of Andrews Liver Salts; I remember the bubbles fizzing up my nose as I drank it. We also had Milk of Magnesia in our cupboard.

For extreme cases of constipation there was Ex-Lax, which looks like a small bar of chocolate. One day when I was younger, I found a bar of this on the mantle shelf and ate half of it. The rest of that day was spent in and out of the toilet, something that taught me a very painful lesson. If there was any sign of a urine infection or backache, we took a Bile Bean capsule, which turned your wee green.

If I grazed a knee or another part of my anatomy, Dad would put a tiny amount of red crystals (called Condy's Crystals) from a jar into very hot water to bathe it. As they dissolved, the liquid turned bright red.

We also had Germolene antiseptic, which was pink and creamy and came in a small round tin with a lid. There was Vaseline and castor oil cream to sooth sore places and calamine lotion for sunburn or rashes. After the calamine dried on your skin, it flaked off when rubbed away. If you had a sore eye, there was a small tube of Golden Eye ointment, which made your eye feel sticky. Dad also had a piece of Alum in what he referred to as Doctor Urry's medical box; I think he used this to dry up blood from small cuts, especially those incurred while shaving. There was also iodine, which turned your skin yellow when applied to cuts. For a sore throat or ulcerated mouth we always used salt water, to either gargle or swill our mouths with. Any family member with aching joints was advised to use Fynnon or Epsom salts – I'm not sure whether they drank it or put it into their bath water, though – and then they used to rub in Lloyd's Cream. If your feet ached, a good soak in a bowl of hot water with mustard in it would be recommended. For a burn, Mum would smear it with butter (not recommended now of course), something that – along with vinegar and sugar – was also used to soothe a cough. If I developed a chesty cough, then my chest and back was smothered in Vick's. This was also put on the outside and inside of a blocked up nose.

I once had a terrible earache when my grandfather was visiting, so he made me sit in front of him with a clean hanky over my ear. He then blew hot smoke from his cigarette into my ear and it somehow cured my earache, although this technique wouldn't be recommended today.

For headaches and colds, we had Aspro, a brand of aspirin that came in long pink strips, and children's aspirin for the young ones. The cough mixture we used was Venos, or else we inhaled steam, with our faces over a bowl of boiled water and a towel over our heads if it affected our chests. My father had a large black medical book, so he could look up any ailments and suggest a cure.

If we wanted professional advice regarding a medical problem, we would go to Tremletts Chemists in New Road, Portsmouth. Tremletts, established in Fratton Road in 1901 by Percy Gordon Tremlett, had several shops in the area. If we were ill during the 1950s, this trusted chemist would be the first port of call.

The doctor we used had been Dad's family doctor for years before, and he seemed quite elderly. The surgery was in a large corner house in Copnor, close to HM Prison Kingston. I think his name was something like Collins or Cooper. You didn't make an appointment then; you just turned up when you were ill and waited your turn. When the NHS was introduced in 1948, all treatment from doctors, dentists and opticians was free to all. From 1952, a prescription charge of 1s (5p) was introduced, with a £1 charge for dental treatment.

Fortunately, I didn't need to visit the hospital often during my childhood. If I had, there were several in Portsmouth in the 1950s. St Mary's Hospital, which was built in 1898, is on Milton Road, where I was born in 1946. The hospital is now just for maternity, dermatology and elderly rehab, although it also has a pain clinic. The Royal Hospital, built in 1848, was in Commercial Road – very convenient for the people living in the city, and close enough to the dockyard for any emergencies or accidents. Unfortunately, it was closed down in 1978 and demolished in 1979. It is now the site for a large Sainsbury's supermarket. Most of the hospital patients in and around Portsmouth now have to visit the Queen Alexandra Hospital in Cosham, which was built in 1908. This hospital is now equipped with all the latest technology and it is the only remaining general hospital in the area.

When I was quite young, it was discovered that I had a lazy eye, and I had to attend the Eye & Ear Hospital in Grove Road, Southsea. This hospital was closed down in 1971 has since been absorbed by Queen Alexandra Hospital.

There is also a psychiatric hospital in Locksway Road, Milton, called St James', which opened in 1878 and remains in operation.

MEALTIMES

Although we didn't have the choice of foods we have now, I felt they were always nourishing and tasty. We always ate our dinner around midday. I did not like school meals and lived close by, so I came home for my dinner. There were no microwaves then, so Dad's meal was heated up on top of a saucepan of boiling water when he came home in the evening.

For family meals we had roast beef, lamb or pork on a Sunday, with seasonal vegetables and delicious Yorkshire puds. The leftover meat would have been made into a Lancashire hotpot or cottage pie, and any vegetables fried with bread and made into bubble and squeak for Monday. The beef was roasted in the oven in lard, and when the meat was cooked, the fat was drained and poured into a china basin. When this dripping was set, the meat juice formed a delicious jelly at the bottom of the basin. We all loved this spread on thickly sliced bread with a sprinkling of salt on top. Gorgeous.

We also ate sausages in batter, toad in the hole, home-made steak and kidney pies and steamed pudding. I remember pig's trotters (which I didn't like), belly pork with crispy crackling and breast of lamb, boned and rolled with sage and onion stuffing.

Tripe was cooked and served in a white onion sauce. We had liver and bacon, in thick Bisto gravy that you could slice with a knife. Neck of lamb, cooked into a stew with pearl barley and fluffy suet dumplings. There was sometimes rabbit stew and oxtail, but chicken in the early 1950s was reserved for Christmas, until we switched to turkey. Another delicacy my parents ate was long, wrinkled looking chiddlings, or pig's intestines, which I did not like the look of and never ate.

At about 5 p.m. we had tea, often thick sliced bread toasted by the fire on a winter's evening, at the end of a long fork. We either ate this plain with butter, or with cheese, beans, jam or egg on top. We also toasted crumpets in the same way smothering these with butter. Teatime was always bread-based, as it was filling.

Cakes were reserved for weekends or if we had guests; then it would be fruit cake, Madeira, Angel cake, Battenberg or Jamaican ginger cake. These were shop bought – Mum was not a baker. At weekends we sometimes had a pudding, or 'afters', as Mum called it. This was homemade apple, gooseberry, rhubarb or jam short pastry tart, with Bird's custard. A spotted dick (suet pudding with dried fruit) was often steamed in a saucepan, wrapped in a clean cloth and served with custard or jam or Tate & Lyle treacle. Sometimes Mum baked large cooking apples in the oven and we smothered these with dried fruit, sugar and custard. Milk puddings were popular – rice, sago or tapioca – and Mum's speciality was a bread pudding so large that it lasted a week.

We all drank tea; even when I was a young child, it was that or water. Soft and fizzy drinks were for holidays and hot summer days. In the evenings, Mum often made us a cup of hot milky Horlicks or Ovaltine; I drank mine from a white mug with an ear for a handle. My favourite hot drink on a cold evening was an Oxo cube dissolved in a cup of boiling water, with thick bread for dipping. If I was unwell, Mum made me hot sweet milk and bought me a bottle of Lucozade with the orange cellophane wrapper (I had all the usual childhood ailments: measles, chickenpox and mumps). Then I spent a few days tucked up in a warm cosy bed with a coal fire blazing in the grate – if it was winter – with a new book and comic and a bunch of grapes to eat. I must admit I loved the TLC I received when I was unwell, and sometimes I made it last longer than it should have done.

KEEPING WARM AND COSY

When I was a child, there was no central heating in the house; only coal fires in some of the rooms that were in use. There were draughts everywhere, so in the winter Dad used to fix a thick curtain over the inside of the front door. He tacked thick rubber draught excluder round the window frames and the front and three back doors. When the weather was freezing, the insides of the windows had ice on them. Every room in the house, except the bathroom and kitchen, had an open fireplace with a chimney. Each fireplace that was used had to be cleaned out every morning and the cinders raked out and removed. It was then relaid, with newspaper, wood and coal, ready to be lit when required. Sometimes Mum or Emily had to hold a large sheet of newspaper in front of the fire when lighting it to stop the draught from the chimney putting the flames out. Often a sharp wind would blow down the chimney and fill the room with smoke. During the day, the fire had to be restocked with shovels of coal taken from a scuttle in the grate.

I also remember a companion set that sat next to the fire. This was a stand with a small shovel, tongs and long poker to stoke the fire with. Whenever anyone came into the room, they seemed to have a poke around the fire with this. I loved to just stare into the flames, imagining scenes and people living in there.

Every so often, the chimney needed to be swept clean of soot, so a chimney sweep was asked to call. Mum and Emily covered the room or rooms with newspaper and old sheets before the sweep arrived, with his brushes and rods already covered in soot from his previous job. Whilst he pushed the brush and rods up the chimney, we all went into the garden to watch until the sooty brush popped out of the pot on top of the roof. When the job was completed and the sweep was on his way, everyone helped to clean up the rooms, removing any traces of soot.

We used a lot of coal in the winter, so Mum used to order a ton of coal – which would be about twenty bags – in the summer, when it was cheaper. I think the coal merchant she used was Fraser & Whites, in Portsmouth. The lorry arrived on the day specified, and as they had to bring the coal through the passage, Mum covered the floor with newspaper. In the garden was a brick-built coal bunker with a chute in the front for the coal to come out and a lid at the top to pour the coal into. Mum always counted the bags in, as she couldn't afford to be one bag short.

DUSTBIN DAY

Every week, the metal dustbin had to be carried from the back garden, through the passage and out the front door to the forecourt, ready for the dustman to empty it. There were no plastic sacks or bin liners, and everything went into that bin, so it was rather smelly. In our household, all vegetable and fruit peelings were put onto a compost heap in the garden, ready to rot down and spread on Mum's vegetable plot. The tea leaves from the strainer that we used in our cups were put into a metal bin with holes in the top. When they were dry, Emily spread these onto the mats and rugs to lift the dust and dirt before she beat them with a broom. Any leftover stale bread was made into puddings, and leftover food was reused the next day, so the bin didn't contain much food; only bones and remains, which were wrapped in newspaper. Old newspaper was also used to clean windows and protect tables when polishing brass and shoes, as well as a base for the coal fires. Glass milk bottles were collected by the milkman each day and drinks bottles had a deposit paid on them, which could be reclaimed when the bottle was returned to the shop or pub. Most things were sold loose in the 1950s and any packaging was paper, not plastic, so tended to be reused rather than just thrown away. Therefore, we had very little to dispose of; a small dustbin was quite sufficient for most household waste.

When the rubbish was collected, the bins were hoisted onto the dustmen's shoulders – sometimes two at a time – and emptied into the dustcart. They all wore headgear similar to the coalman, with a veil to cover the back of their necks and leather shoulder pads. I think they also tied rope or elastic round the bottom of their trousers to protect them from any rats that might be amongst the rubbish.

HOBBIES

Next to the kitchen was the living room, and it usually lived up to the name, as we did everything in this room. There was a coal fire, which all the family sat around when it was cold, with armchairs and dining chairs around the hearth. There was also a large wooden dining table in here, which could be extended by pulling out extra leaves that slid underneath when not in use. All family meals were eaten on this table, which was also used for ironing and doing various hobbies.

My mother loved jigsaws, so there was always one on the go, resting on a board. She was also an avid cinemagoer and collected pictures of her favourite stars from several film magazines, pasting them into scrap books. She found these in magazines such as *Picturegoer*, *Life* and *Movie Stars*. I spent my evenings drawing, painting, attempting colouring-in books and putting together cut-out cardboard dolls with a selection of assorted clothes that attached at the shoulder. There were also stencil sets, Plasticine to mould into shapes and potato man pieces to make a face. For this I needed a large raw potato, and it sometimes ended up in a toy box, only to be brought out later in the year, covered in roots. We also played board games together: we had a Monopoly set and an old game of Lotto (bingo). The counters were made of wood, and those I still have today, as well as the large cardboard bingo cards. We also had a 'compendium of games', which included Snakes & Ladders, Ludo, Draughts and a small game of Roulette. Sometimes Mum got her large heavy slate shove halfpenny board out and we would have a few games on the dining table. On the back of the living room door we sometimes hung a dartboard, so Dad could have a game with my uncles when they were visiting.

Whilst sitting in his armchair by the fire, my father made his own workbags by cutting out a pattern in leather and sewing this together with thick twine, which was soaked in some kind of awful-smelling grease. He did all the household mending,

Portsmouth football team in the 1950s.

as Mum didn't sew, and I remember him darning his woollen socks by fitting them over a sort of wooden mushroom. He also read loads of paperback cowboy stories. Dad didn't gamble on horses or anything like that, but he loved to do the football pools every week. He turned this into a hobby, as he studied the advice given in several newspapers before he made his selection. There was a range – Littlewoods Copes and Vernon's Pools among them – and he did them all. On Saturdays, we all had to be very quiet whilst he listened to the results on the radio. The most he ever won was £25, but he enjoyed the thrill of it all.

Both my parents loved watching or listening to sport: my mother loved cricket, tennis and horse racing. Dad's favourite sports were boxing and football. His first love was, of course, his home team Pompey, the team he supported all through his life. The club was formed at Fratton Park in 1898 with John Brickwoods, who owned the local Brickwoods Brewery, as their chairman. I can still remember a few players from the 1950s:

Tommy McChee, a full-back who played for Portsmouth between 1954 and 1959.

Duggie Reid, an inside forward from 1946 until 1956.

Jackie Henderson, who played as centre forward, inside forward and winger for Pompey from 1949 until 1958.

Jack Froggatt, left half between 1946 and 1954.

Reg Flewin the brother of Dad's friend Fred Flewin. Reg was a central defender who played for Portsmouth from 1937 until 1953.

Jimmy Dickinson, playing between 1946 and 1964 as a left half.

Pompey Football club enjoyed a very successful 2007–08 Premier League season, when they won the FA Cup, beating Cardiff 1–0. However, the club encountered financial problems and they were relegated to League Two, being declared bankrupt in 2013. They are now owned by the fans and supporters.

—

We played Snakes and Ladders, five stones and snap. For toys I liked dolls and a pram, also a plastic tea set.

Margaret Thomas, née Gilkerson

Margaret Gilkerson. This photograph was taken around 1950 in Portsmouth.

I didn't have many toys – just dolls and board games, such as Snakes and Ladders. We played in the street mostly; hide and seek, ball games and skipping. I soon learnt to knit and sew, taught by my mum, Vera Organ, and I loved reading.

Jean Palmer, née Organ

We played Snakes and Ladders, cards and five stones and hide and seek in the air raid shelter. My dad, Charles, built me a large wooden plane and a boat to play with too.

Tony Thomas

Tony Thomas with the boat made by his father.

I played hopscotch, five stones marbles, skipping on my own and with a long rope with other children in the street. We also played 'round and round the elephant's back', hide and seek, conkers, cat's cradle with a length of wool, and I had a yo-yo too. I also loved playing musical dancing and Cinderella and Prince Charming. I had roller skates, a post office set, a nurse's outfit and a bus conductor set with tickets. I was taken to the roller skating rink and I enjoyed riding my bike.

Diane Williams, née LeMettey

We played with marbles in the gutter, as there were hardly any cars in the street. After school we all went to the recreation ground to meet other boys and girls for a chat. Later in the '50s, we focused on the dating game.

Then there was the Omo launch. Our gang of three would meet up in our 'den' in the garden of our Newcome Road house every Sunday morning. One particular week, small packets of Omo washing powder were left on the doorsteps of neighbouring houses as a promotion. We were prompted by this to wash the sacking seat covers on the benches in our den, so we gathered up all the packets of Omo from the doorsteps nearby and washed the sacking. My parents were out for the day, so I decided to hang the sacking on the fireguard in front of the fire to dry. An hour later I checked to see if the sacking was dry, to be met by a room full of dense smoke and scorched sacking. We opened doors and windows and threw the sacks out, but the smell still lingered. When our parents returned, our faces were a picture of innocence as to what was causing the smell, as we had been busy in the den.

Ken Matthews

Doreen Linsdale with her sister Linda and cousin Margaret Gilkerson.

I enjoyed playing shops, hospitals, marbles, hopscotch and riding my bike. I also had a walkie-talkie doll and a pram. Later in the '50s I enjoyed going to the cinema and we used to go to a cafe to listen to records on the jukebox. I loved reading too.

Doreen Matthews, née Linsdale

two

SHOPS AND FOOD

As my parents didn't own a refrigerator, we had to shop daily, except for Sundays, when most shops were closed. Milk and bread was delivered, and a Corona soft drinks lorry also came round the houses now and again. From this you could buy bottles of lemonade, Tizer, ginger beer, American cream soda and cherryade, as well as a range of other soft drinks. In the summer, Mum sometimes bought a bottle of cream soda and a block of ice cream to put a dollop in the glass – delicious.

SHOPPING IN CHICHESTER ROAD

My mother did all her other shopping locally, as we didn't have a car. If you turned to your left as you came out of my road and walked along Chichester Road, you would have come to the Co-operative food store. Mum shopped here for her store cupboard groceries. As she used the Co-op milkman and bakery delivery, Mum would have bought the tokens here to pay at the end of the week, using her dividend number. I think blue tokens were for milk and red for bread. The 'divi', as most people called it, was a small share of the Co-op's profits, paid to its customers just before Christmas each year. It depended on how much a customer spent in their stores, and there were several in Portsmouth then. As well as food, there was a Co-op department store in Fratton which sold most things, including furniture. It was here that Mum collected her 'divi' and probably spent most of it on Christmas gifts in the store. This large Co-op store is now closed, and the site is occupied by the Bridge Shopping Centre.

THE BASICS

Close to the Co-op in Chichester Road was a greengrocer's named Hayters. Mr Hayter, the owner, was a well-built man with a chubby face, receding hair and glasses with thick lenses like bottle bases that made his eyes look tiny. He always wore a long, dark grey overall and was very pleasant to everyone; he knew most of his customers by name. His shop was quite dark inside, with just one small bulb giving out light. At the front of the shop, all the vegetables, fruit and salads were laid out in wooden boxes, stood on a piece of imitation grass. In the 1950s the availability of produce depended on the season. In winter, there was usually a pile of tied-up bundles of chopped firewood for sale.

We didn't have the choice of food like we do now, but at least most of it was fresh and produced in this country. Mum grew a few vegetables and salads, but the garden wasn't large enough to keep the family fed all year round. I remember mainly eating dark greens or cabbage, marrow, swede and cauliflower and broad beans and peas. Carrots and turnips were only used in stews in our house, not as a side vegetable, and swede was always mashed with potato. If Mum had a cold in the winter, she would throw a large onion into the flames of the coal fire until the skin turned black, then peel it and eat the onion like an apple.

The only time we had a large bowl of fruit was at Christmas; other than that, it was only when in season. There was usually a large, juicy orange, which Dad would peel and share. He always cut up all the fruit he ate. Grapes were only bought if someone was ill, and they had loads of pips in them. We had bananas sliced with custard and apple or rhubarb as pudding, either plain or under pastry.

Inside the shop, Mr Hayter sold a small selection of groceries, and he had a slicing machine on the counter for cold meats and bacon. Cheese was sliced with a wire cutter. At the front of the counter was a stand which had large tins of loose biscuits, with glass lids displaying the variety: Rich Tea, digestive, ginger nuts, custard creams and Nice biscuits, with one tin holding broken biscuits at a reduced price. These would all be weighed out and put into paper bags. In the few weeks before Christmas, Mr Hayter had a few Christmas trees, as well as holly and mistletoe, for sale. He must have had a tank of paraffin at the back of his shop as well, as you could take a can or bottle in to have it filled up for your oil heater.

From a very young age I was sent out with a large shopping bag (that dragged on the floor as I was so small), to collect a few things Mum had forgotten to buy. I would be given a list, with the money tightly wrapped inside. Mr Hayter or his assistant filled my bag and wrapped the change in the list to take back to Mum. I remember being given stern warnings by

Mum, Gran and Emily to never talk to strangers, so I always walked with my face down, terrified that someone might try to grab me.

A bit further on from this was a fish and chip shop that was indistinguishable from the houses around it, and this was always very popular. You could smell the delicious aroma as you walked along; I think they used lard or dripping instead of oil. Across the road was the post office, which was also operated as a newsagent. Coming back down the road, was a small sweet shop; I didn't use this one as I would have had to cross over the road. There were two public houses along Chichester Road; the Lord Chichester and the Pelham, and opposite the Pelham was another fish and chip shop. We only occasionally had fish and chips; Mum usually fried the meal herself, as it was cheaper. When I was still in a pushchair, sometimes Emily would take me over to the one near the Pelham and buy me two pennies (two pennuth) worth of chips, wrapped in a greaseproof paper bag and newspaper.

When we turned out of our road to the right, there was Hawkins, the butchers, where Mum bought all her meat. One of the butchers there was called John and he looked the part; well fed with a large rosy freckled face and a bald head. He also knew his customers by name, and was rather saucy with all the ladies, which they seemed to enjoy. The floor of the shop was covered in sawdust, and the heavy wooden counters were used to chop and slice up the various animals, spilling the blood onto the floor. There was a large walk-in fridge along one wall, and meat on display, hanging on metal hooks around the window. There were also long chains of sausages made on the premises, trays of various meats, including a large tray of creamy tripe and one of pig's trotters, both favourites of my mothers. A few chickens were hung up with their heads and feet still on and a few feathers left to pluck, alongside rabbits still in their fur skins, hung upside-down, waiting to be someone's dinner.

Not far away was a gentlemen's tailor shop, and my father had his best suit made there. His hats and accessories were bought in Dunn's outfitters in Commercial Road, Portsmouth. They used to put his initials inside his hats, which he loved.

There was an electrical shop near our road, selling small electric appliances and plugs and bulbs. One Christmas, my parents bought a set of coloured tree lights in this shop. They were large screw in bulbs in different colours and shapes; some were snowmen and Father Christmas heads. We had them for years, as you could replace the screw in bulbs. Our house didn't have many electrical sockets in the wall, so when Mum eventually bought an electric iron she used to plug it into the light bulb socket. It seems dangerous now, but you could buy a two-way ceiling socket to hang from the wire, and the iron was fitted with a plug that went into this contraption, next to the bulb. Mum hated dark rooms and she used an enormous 150-watt light bulb in the living room.

Clothes were repaired and shoes mended by my father. New things were bought only for special occasions. Mum wasn't interested in new clothes for everyday wear, so wore the same casual things for years. A couple of summer dresses and slacks and tops in the winter were all she required. Dad was very fussy about his clothes for best, and Mum liked him to look good, as he was a handsome man, so would order him a new suit every few years.

His shirts were always pure white and starched, and his best ones were laundered at Chapman's Laundry. Dad had a variety of hats and ties with a selection of his favourite bow ties including a fun one that lit up that he wore at parties. He also had a trilby for work and a new one for going out, a straw one for the summer and a sporty one with a feather in the side for casual occasions. He also had an old black Humber that he called his 'Antony Eden hat'. According to Dad, flat caps were only ever worn in the garden. In the winter he always wore a night cap like Wee Willy Winky, as he maintained that a lot of body heat escapes through your head. He had a full head of hair until he died, so it clearly didn't make his hair fall out, as Mum said it would.

I had a completely new outfit bought for me at Whitsun (spring bank holiday), sometimes a dress, with an occasional summer coat and hat, and maybe a pair of white buckskin sandals that could be whitened with Blanco. I always longed for a pair of black patent slip-on shoes like my cousin Diane had, but Dad always insisted that my shoes must have straps or laces. I once persuaded Mum to buy me a pair of red slip-on shoes, and I was so proud of them. When my father saw them, he took them into his shed and made straps with red leather and attached these to my new shoes. Dad used to be a ballroom dancer and wore patent shoes which ruined his feet and deformed his toes, so he didn't want me to suffer too. I wasn't impressed at the time; I am grateful to him now though.

Just before my birthday in November, I usually had a new party dress, which would last until the following year. I wore my school uniform all week and last year's clothes for weekends, keeping my set of new clothes for best. Underwear was not changed daily, as it is now, so we didn't need so many. For bed, I wore winceyette pyjamas or a nightie.

Girls had to wear skirts to school and boys short trousers. It got rather chilly in winter, so we must have been a hardy lot. I had brown Clark's sandals in the summer for school and shoes with buckles in the winter, although I did also own a pair of black wellington boots for the snow and rain. They were worn with socks, not tights, so when it rained, the inside of my legs would get red and raw with the wet and cold. My navy blue gabardine mac lasted until the hem reached my bottom. I remember that I had mittens on a piece of wool threaded through my sleeves, so they couldn't be lost. The woollen hat I wore was on a metal band to keep it on my head, with a large pompom at the back. The boys used to grab these off your head as they ran past and throw them in the hedge. I thumped a boy called Brian Lamb for taking mine. There was also a fashion to wear a long woollen scarf knitted in spider stitch, with large pompoms at each end in various colours. My mother couldn't knit, so I was delighted when one of Emily's nieces made one for me and I wore it till it fell to bits.

LUXURIES

Not far from the butcher's was Martin's sweet shop and newsagent. This became especially popular once the sweet rations were abandoned. We didn't have sweets on a daily basis, though: it was usually at the weekends, or when family came to visit. My mother's favourites were the creamy white milk bottles, coconut mushrooms, caramel teacakes, marshmallow and nougat. Dad, for his part, always had a small tin of Black Imps mints in his pocket. If I had a few pennies to spare, I bought a selection of four for a penny (a farthing each), usually black jacks, pink shrimp, fruit chews, or some everlasting toffee that got stuck in your teeth. There were also long strings of liquorice, packets of sweet cigarettes and loose dolly mixture; aniseed balls, pear drops, liquorice allsorts and Sharp's toffees. Most of the sweets were in large glass jars displayed on a shelf, which were weighed in anything from a couple of ounces upwards. There were also bars of chocolate and I loved Fry's chocolate cream. Sometimes Mum bought a small quarter pound box of Dairy Box to share in the evening. Martin's also sold ice cream. As we didn't have a freezer, Mum would buy an oblong bar of vanilla ice cream and a packet of wafers, which we had to use up quickly before it melted. As a Christmas treat, my stocking sometimes contained a box with a chocolate pipe, cigars and lighter, or a Father Christmas figure which I would be reluctant to eat. Martin's also sold soft drinks and Mum enjoyed a glass of Robinsons' lemon barley water. She bought it as she said it was 'good for the system'.

We had newspapers and comics delivered most days of the week. Every morning we received the *Daily Sketch* and the *Portsmouth Evening News* was delivered in the evening. If Granddad was visiting, he always read the *Daily Herald*. On Saturday, Dad used to buy the *Sports Mail*, also known as 'the pinkie', due to the colour. On the front was a cartoon face of a sailor, and if Portsmouth FC won he had his thumbs up; across and it was a draw, and down meant that they had lost. My father and most male members of the family supported Portsmouth. They went to the local match at Fratton Park and some of the important away matches too. On Sunday, Mum and Dad read the *Sunday People* and the *News of the World*. When we had a television, Mum bought the *Radio Times* each week, along with her film magazines.

My delivery of comics was very welcome as we didn't own many books; I only had the Christmas annuals and a few Disney fairy stories to read. Instead, I would look forward to my delivery of *Dandy, Beano, Beezer, Bunty, Topper, Girl* and also *Eagle* (intended for boys, but Mum enjoyed reading it). I loved the free gifts such as paper bangers, jewellery and plastic figures. When I was very young, I remember a comic called *Playbox* and also another called *Radio Fun*, which consisted of cartoons featuring characters from radio programmes.

Woolworths had an entrance on Chichester Road, and you walked through and came out another door into London Road, North End. Woolworths was quite dark inside, as it lacked windows and had bare brown varnished floorboards. All the counters had an assistant in burgundy overalls, standing in the middle, surrounded by goods displayed in sections laid out flat so you could handle the item. At the back of each item was a square chrome display stand with a red sign depicting the prices, which were usually just a few pennies or shillings per item. There were tools, jewellery, toys, make-up and reading spectacles. I remember seeing colourful tin buckets and spades and large rubber balls, ready to take to our local beach in Southsea. You could buy small plastic household gadgets for just a few shillings, as well as cutlery, crockery and ornaments. In 1959, I bought my mum an amber-coloured glass vase, and I still have it in my sitting room. They sold sweets, biscuits and slabs of cake sold by the weight. Knitting wool and haberdashery were all on display, at a fraction of the price in the bigger stores. At Christmas, there was a large counter given over to decorations, lights and Christmas crackers. As a child I did all my Christmas shopping there after saving up my small amount of pocket money. Woolworths sold a variety of goods and was perfect for anyone on a low income, especially children with just a few pennies to spend.

NORTH END

Another large store in North End was Will Brown's haberdashery shop. In here you could buy material cut to the required length, along with everything required to make a new outfit. They also sold chair backs, cushions and general haberdashery. When you paid for an item, the money was put into a metal and glass tube and sent flying through on a wire to the cashier in the office, who sent the change and receipt back to the counter.

When Will Brown's disappeared from London Road, it was replaced by another haberdashery store called Bulpitts, a modern store set up where the old Woolworths used to be. A larger Woolworths therefore took up a new location, further up the High Street.

Belmont's was an exclusive shop, selling women's designer clothing. Mum would stare longingly in the window, wishing she could afford the beautiful clothes on display. Her wish eventually came true, as in 1965 she bought a gold lamé suit in there for my wedding and looked wonderful in it. This shop is sadly no longer trading in Portsmouth.

There was a small café called The Cup and Saucer, and my friends and I spent many hours in here as teenagers, drinking frothy coffee out of a glass cup and saucer. That disappeared years ago.

If Mum was shopping for food in North End she often bought bread and cakes from Smith and Vosper bakery. She also used David Grieg, a lovely fresh and clean store selling cheeses, cold meats, eggs and other dairy products. This was on large counters, with the assistants dressed in white overalls ready to serve you the required product. Along London Road there was a dry-cleaner's, and in the window sat a lady who used to repair stockings. She might have sewn other things, but I only saw her with stockings in her hand; I think it was called 'invisible mending'. A very posh-looking hairdresser, called Andrea, owned premises next door and my mother told me that the lady who owned this was in the bed next to her in hospital and that her baby was born on the same day as me. In the window there used to be beautiful jewellery and make-up on display.

Just past the Odeon cinema was the Clarence Gardens pub, and on the corner was a department store. McElroy's was another department store a bit further on, but this company no longer exists. Verrichia's ice cream parlour was another favourite place to visit. Here you could sit and have an banana split or ice cream sundae, or take a lovely ice cream cone with you to eat along the way. Another pub called the Green Post was on the way out of North End. On the corner of High Street and Gladys Avenue was the Southdown Coach travel agents. This was where Mum went to book a day out on a coach in the summer.

Coming back down the High Street, there was Rumblows, an electrical retailer. You would then pass Dewhurst butchers, a fruit and veg shop, a chemist and the Thatched House pub. On another corner was St Mark's church, where there was usually a wedding brightening up the street on a Saturday. I was married in this church in the 1960s and so were several of my friends. Sadly the lovely old St Mark's church was eventually demolished and a modern church built opposite in Derby Road. A Co-operative is on the old site at the time of writing.

The Gaumont cinema was on the same side of the street, as well as Marks & Spencer, where Mum bought some of my clothes. My school uniform would have been from M&S; a white cotton blouse with grey pleated skirt and grey or red cardigan. I worked in that branch of Marks & Spencer in the '60s, wearing the smart blue and white checked dress with a belt. I was so happy to be working there and wore my gold-coloured M&S badge on my collar with pride. Unfortunately, this store ultimately left North End shopping centre and another clothing store with lower priced stock is now in its place.

Slapes was a wet fish shop; Mum must have used this often as the family loved fish, especially if it was fresh. The selection of fish was laid out on a sloping display facing into the street, including plaice, cod, skate, smoked haddock, herrings and mackerel, bass and trout. The assistants always looked cold, with their black wellington boots and rubber aprons on, their hands red and raw in the open air. My mum especially loved the shellfish, crab, and lobster, although she was also very fond of jellied eels. There were several fishermen in her mother's side of the family, the Clarks. One of her cousins once brought round a large tin bath full of eels still wriggling about in the water.

Slapes sold prawns, cockles, mussels and winkles by the pint glass full. We often had winkles for Sunday tea with bread and butter. On the plate would be a pin or needle to dig into the tiny grey shell and pull the winkle out, first removing the small black cover. My father used to cover his face with these, pretending he had a disease, or he would put one on his cheek, like a beauty spot.

Campion's, the baker's, stood on a corner. This shop was later replaced by a clothing store. At 15 years of age, I started work in Campion's bakers in Fratton Road, Portsmouth, earning the grand sum of £2 2s 3d per week. I didn't pass any exams at school, but by working hard and demonstrating my ambition, I was promoted to the position of manager at the age of 17, thus increasing my pay to £9.

Next door was Freeman, Hardy & Willis, a shoe shop, and above one of the shops was a hairdresser called Charles of Bond Street, which I used as a teenager.

I attended Sunday school in the adjacent London Road Baptist Church and I still have my small bible and prayer book from that time. This church has now been transformed into a pub called Lanyards.

There were lots of other little shops that I cannot remember; I may not have been into them. Past the Blue Anchor pub, going into Kingston Crescent, was a small gift shop named The Wishing Well. If I had saved enough money, I would buy a small present for Mum in here for Christmas or a birthday, as they were of a better quality than Woolworths. Opposite this shop was the Essoldo cinema and the White Hart pub, which stood on the corner. The building was later taken over by an insurance company.

There was another shopping centre in Commercial Road, but we only used that if we wished to buy clothes in C&A or Newman. If we wanted to visit a market we would go to Charlotte Street. This was a large, noisy, bustling place, selling fruit, veg and meat, plus various stalls selling cheaper versions of toys, clothes, jewellery and bric-a-brac. Other businesses in Charlotte Street were Franks, G.A. Walters Refreshment Room and Restaurant, Dick Keech & Son Naval Tailors and Cox's Hotel. There was also Little Charlotte Street. Shipps greengrocer and Shirt King were once situated on Meadow Street, going into Charlotte Street (named after the wife of George III), but that road no longer exists.

On Commercial Road, one would find W. Barratts and G.W. Morton, both functioning as boot makers, Murdock musical instruments, and J.M. Store, a radio dealer. There was then a turn off towards Crasswell Street, and on the other corner was Halfords bicycle builders (at that time, Halfords trained young engineers). There was also the Duke of York pub; this closed down in 1953. Next to Boots, the chemist, was J. Lyons Restaurant, H.J. Wilson, costumier, Phillips Store Ltd, house furnishers, and Rego, clothiers. The Landport Drapery Bazaar, known as the LDB, was founded in 1865 and destroyed by bombs during the Second World War. The current building, constructed in the early 1950s, was damaged by fire in 1965. It was taken over by Allders in 1982 and has been Debenhams since 2005. I remember visiting a café above a shop in Commercial Road called The Black Cat Café, on the rare occasions we went out to eat.

There were also shops in Palmerston Road, Southsea, but they were sometimes a bit pricey. My Auntie May sometimes took me to Handleys department store, where we would have afternoon tea and watch the models putting on a fashion show. Auntie used to try on all the perfumes and scented talc on display and this embarrassed me a bit, but she didn't care.

In the middle of every main road junction in Portsmouth there would be a policeman in full uniform and white gloves, directing the traffic; we didn't have the green man guiding us across the road then. From about 1953, the roads outside most schools were patrolled by a lollipop man or lady, to help the children across safely. They wore a white coat and their sign was a rectangle, painted red and black with the words 'STOP: CHILDREN CROSSING'.

The policeman was a reassuring presence who could also help with an accident and keep the traffic flowing at a steady pace too. You were always sure to see a policeman on his beat patrolling the streets, too. It was usually enough of a deterrent for most young people having an argument or ready for a fight to walk away and cool down. The policeman was there to give advice and stop a crime before it happened. He would be in full uniform with the standard police helmet on. He had a whistle to blow to summon help and a truncheon with which to defend himself. The woman's uniform was similar, but with a skirt instead of trousers. I don't remember seeing a woman officer patrolling the streets in Portsmouth when I was a child, so maybe they were office-based then. My family and I were never in any kind of trouble with the law, so we were a bit in awe of any policemen we saw. We didn't own anything of value, so were not likely to be the victim of a burglary, but I was always told to find a policeman if I was ever lost or in trouble, so felt a certain trust in them. The police sometimes rode a bike, or for a serious crime a big black car or van was used, which everyone called a Black Maria. The main streets had blue boxes on some corners, which were only for the police to use.

Most of the shops in North End have changed so frequently over the years that I no longer recognise the High Street; it is not the same place I enjoyed shopping in during the '50s. There is no cinema to visit, and all the big high street names have since moved on to larger premises.

—

As teenagers we used to go to a record shop called Weston Harts in the city centre; we all went into the record booth to listen to the latest hits. After that, it would be over to Verrichia's ice cream café, by the town train station.

In 1959 I left school and took the Dockyard Apprentice exam and passed, to start work in January 1960. Between leaving school and starting in the dockyard, I took a job in the Landport Drapery Bazaar (LDB). Whilst I worked there, they also had a warehouse at the top end of Commercial Road which used to be Papps, a music and piano shop. The LDB used to store toys on the top floor, lino and carpets on the ground floor and fireworks in the basement. This wouldn't be allowed now with the health and safety rules.

Other shops I remember were in Tangier Road … Pinks the grocer, and Haskell & Greens record shop in Lake Road.

We had potatoes and veg from Granddad's allotment, bread and jam and homemade soups at home. I remember wearing short trousers and coloured tops.

Tony Thomas

[I remember] going to the C&A store in Commercial Road, Stead & Simpson shoe shop, Woolworth, Littlewoods and Landports and Smiths.

I wore can-can petticoats, full skirts and dresses, suits with a skirt and Italian striped pencil skirts [and] Whispy shoes, which were stilettoes with very pointed toes.

The food I remember was winkles, cockles, kidneys and stuffed hearts, liver bacon and onions. Chicken in a basket with chips and ploughman's lunch in Dad's pub. We also often went out for Chinese meals.

Diane Williams, née LeMettey

I went to C&A in Commercial Road and Woolworths, David Grieg's and Sainsbury's.

I enjoyed bread and jam, potatoes, soups and steamed puddings. I remember wearing hand-knitted jumpers and pinafore dresses.

Margaret Thomas, née Gilkerson

There were several corner shops, the Co-op supermarket and we had veggies delivered by horse and cart. The food I remember is tripe and onions, cockles and winkles and Yorkshire pud with jam on.

I wore my brown school uniform in the week. Then there was tight skirts, dirndl skirts, polo jumpers and Picture Frame heeled shoes. I wore nylon stockings, which could be mended if laddered.

Doreen Matthews, née Linsdale

We had a convenience store in Newcomen Road, where I lived; it was called Handy Stores. Sunday always saw us having a roast dinner with beef, pork, veal or chicken. Dad would make an 'oosh-ma-koosh', which was a glorified omelette with all sorts thrown in. Monday till Friday, I had school dinners.

I had my first business venture as a boy, when a friend and I asked the vicar of St Mary's church in Fratton if we could use a large workshop to put together some bicycles. He agreed, and we collected spare parts from the local tip and built the bikes.

The vicar was horrified when he passed by a few weeks later to find people coming off the street to buy our bicycles. He closed us down there and then; pity he didn't need a bike.

Ken Matthews

We didn't have supermarkets; there was a butcher and a baker's shop. When I was young, food was still rationed. Although all our food was wholesome and similar to what we eat today, it was all cooked from fresh then. The veg was from the greengrocer. We had sausages and mince, but Mum minced it herself. There were also suet puddings and rice and macaroni puddings too.

Jean Palmer, née Organ

[John lived in Havant Road which was at the back of London Road, North End.]
There was a greengrocer's shop in London Road, and the garage of the shop backed into our road. All the fruit and veg was stored in here and some of the potatoes were old and had roots growing out of them. The owner of the shop asked us kids to pick out all the roots and eyes off the potatoes, and he used to give us bags of fruit for doing this. This was good, as fruit was expensive after the war years.

John Organ

three

ENTERTAINMENT

DANCING IN THE '50s

There were several dance halls in Portsmouth in the 1950s.

The Savoy Ballroom was in South Parade, Southsea, opposite the pier. This was initially for ballroom dancing, attracting all the big names such as Ted Heath, Joe Loss, Chris Barber and Kenny Ball. Acker Bilk was a regular performer there, and also Johnny Dankworth. Several popular vocalists of the day performed at the Savoy, such as Dickie Valentine, Lita Rosa and Dennis Lotis. In the 1960s, the new pop groups appeared at the Savoy including the Beatles, the Rolling Stones and the Kinks. It really was the place to go for a fun night out. It later became a nightclub; first Nero's, then Fifth Avenue, but tastes changed a great deal in the 1990s and the building was eventually demolished.

Kimble's Ballroom in Osborne Road was smaller than the Savoy and had local bands playing, such as Vic Abbot's Palais Nights. In the 1960s, rock groups such as Barry and the

Ballroom dancing at the Savoy, Portsmouth. (*Yesterday Magazine*)

Strollers, the Fleetwoods and the Cadillacs played there. Later The Birdcage Club opened at Kimble's, with performers such as Rod Stewart, the Moody Blues and the T-Bones. Later in the 1960s, it became the Blue Lagoon Club. In the 1970s it was the British Playboy Club (Bunny Club). It is now a casino called the Grosvenor.

The Mecca Locarno Ballroom in Arundel Street also featured big bands, such as the Jack Hawkins Band and the Mel Douglas Set. In the early days, bingo was played in the ballroom. The Mecca eventually became a disco called Ritzy's and is now a fitness centre.

Below the ballroom there was a tenpin bowling alley called 'Ambassador Lanes'. This was later changed to 'Portsmouth Bowl', which was very popular in the 1960s and '70s.

AN EVENING AT THE PICTURES

My parents and I loved going to the cinema, and in the 1950s
it was an inexpensive form of entertainment. In our cinemas
in Portsmouth, you could sit in the front stalls for as little as
1s 9d (about 9p today). This was a bit close to the screen, so for
2s 3d (roughly 11p), you sat further back. When I went with
Mum and Dad, we went upstairs to the posh seats at 3s 6d
(equal to 17½p).

Whenever I accompanied my parents to the Odeon in
London Road, it was always a night out, so we put on our best
clothes, as we were going upstairs to the dress circle. There was
always a queue to get in and the concierge (doorman) stood
in front of us to keep everyone in order. He wore burgundy
trousers and long jacket with gold epaulettes on each shoulder.
With his matching peaked cap, he looked like the captain of the
ship. When he opened up the white rope, we filed through to
pay for our tickets at the square kiosk in the middle. We then
had to climb up the plush red carpeted stairs with its gleaming
brass bannister rail to the dress circle. The usherette, also in
a burgundy suit and with a pillbox hat perched on her head,
would lead us to our seats. She had a large torch to lead you
down, as it was so dark inside. Mum always insisted on sitting at
the front overlooking the balcony, so nobody could sit in front
blocking our view. Dad was deaf in one ear, so he sat on the
end seat as there was a facility for the hard of hearing there.
The seats were red velvet and so was the balcony rail.

Mum sometimes brought a flask of tea and some fruit
with her, plus a bag of sweets to share – after all, it was a
long evening. There used to be a B-movie shown first, then a
cartoon, followed by the Pathé News before the main feature
film. Rather like a theatre performance, there was an interval

when the lights came on and there was usually music, played by Mantovani. The usherette stood at the front of the cinema with a huge tray in front of her, full of ice cream tubs, choc ices, Lyons Maid orange ice lollies and cartons of drinks. Mum bought us all something from the tray and there was enough time to visit the toilet before the main film started. At the end of the film some people tried to rush out before the national anthem was played. But my father was very patriotic and stood to attention like a soldier, saluting his king (and then the queen from 1952), singing every word to the song until it was finished.

There were hundreds of different films on in the 1950s to suit all tastes and age groups; you could spend the week going to the showing of various films at different cinemas in the Portsmouth area. If you went to a late afternoon show you could stay in your seat and watch it all again, because nobody told you to go. You were also allowed to go in halfway between some films and then watch the beginning on the later showing.

I remember some of my favourite films. I had a childish crush on Tony Curtis, so all his films were a must-see, as far as I was concerned, such as *Trapeze* and *Some Like it Hot*, which also starred Marilyn Monroe and Jack Lemmon. I also loved Danny Kaye, so really enjoyed *Hans Christian Anderson*, about the storyteller from Copenhagen. He also starred in *White Christmas* with Bing Crosby, Rosemary Clooney and Vera Allen. Like all children in the '50s, I was of course a fan of any Walt Disney cartoon such as *Cinderella, Lady and the Tramp* and *Snow White*.

- The Odeon, in North End, Portsmouth, opened in 1936. It was a very plush cinema, which made for a very pleasant evening out. This cinema in London Road closed in 2008 and in its place is a Sainsbury's.

- The Gaumont was where I enjoyed my Saturday morning Picture Club in the '50s. It started out as the Regent in 1923, changed to the Gaumont in 1953 and was closed down in 1973.
- The Essoldo in Kingston Crescent was originally known as the Majestic. It became the Essoldo in 1946 but is no longer a cinema, although the building is still standing and was last used as a martial arts centre.
- The Shaftesbury was originally a congregational church and was converted to the Picture Palace in 1915. The cinema closed down in 1959 and became a bingo hall. In 1969, it changed back to a cinema called the Tatler, changing again in 1973 to become the Vogue, then the Classic and finally the Mecca. It is now a bingo hall again. There used to be a large green dome on the roof of the Shaftesbury with a statue of Eros perched on top, but poor old Eros has since disappeared.

The Shaftesbury cinema, with Eros on top of the dome. (*Yesterday Magazine*)

- The Savoy was another very popular cinema in the '50s. It was built in 1937 and changed its name to the ABC in 1964. This cinema was closed in 1999 and demolished in 2002.
- The Troxy was originally the Tivoli when it opened in 1936, but became the Troxy in 1937, remaining such until 1940, when it was closed down. It then became a bingo hall and a discount store. I went to the Troxy once to see Cliff Richard and the Shadows perform there live on stage. In 1996, it was converted into the Kidderminster footwear store.
- The Cinenews, a news theatre, opened in 1936 on Commercial Road (near Dunn's men's outfitters). I sometimes went there during my teenage years, when it was called the Classic, as they showed non-stop cartoons. It went on to show late-night horror films and was closed in 1972.

—

I used to go to the Tivoli cinema, which was in Copnor Road, accompanied by my mum and grandmother. There were once over fifty cinemas and theatres in Portsmouth, now only two cinemas and two theatres remain.

Tony Thomas

SATURDAY MORNING PICTURE CLUB

On Saturday morning, the Gaumont cinema in North End held a children's club, which must have pleased all our parents very much. For 6d, Margaret and I were entertained for a few hours. We all made a tremendous din – screaming, pushing and shoving our way to the seats and shouting and booing the films shown. The hero, who might have been Roy Rogers or Hopalong Cassidy,

The Gaumont cinema, where my friends and I attended the G.P. club in the '50s.
(*Yesterday Magazine*)

was cheered and the baddie booed, and if our hero ever kissed a girl we would all exclaim, 'Yuk!' There was a feature film, a cartoon, children's newsreel and a serial, which always ended with our hero either hanging off a cliff or lying in front of a train. We had to come back the following week to find out if he was saved, which of course he was. In the interval we all sang the club's song which was displayed on the screen in front of us with a dot going along the words. It went something like this …

We come along on Saturday morning, greeting everybody with a
   smile,
We come along on Saturday morning, knowing it is well worthwhile.
All members of the GP club we all intend to be,
Good citizens when we grow up and followers of the free.
We come along on Saturday morning, greeting everybody with a
   smile, smile, smile,
Greeting everybody with a smile.

We ended the song with loud yells and stamping of feet. This must have been a great stress-buster for all of us, after being quiet in school all week.

When you had a birthday, you were sent a birthday card with two free tickets for the following Saturday, so you could take a friend. The whole cinema sang 'Happy Birthday', while your names came up on the screen.

RADIO TIMES

Up until the Coronation in 1953, we only had the radio for home entertainment plus Mum's record collection, which she played on a radiogram. She bought this on hire purchase, but we didn't have it long, as when she was a bit short of cash it had to go back to the shop. Whilst it was in our house, she could listen to all her favourite music on her 78rpm records. I remember that she particularly enjoyed the Glen Miller orchestra, Al Jolson and Winifred Atwell on her honky tonk piano.

Near the end of the 1950s, my parents bought me a red Dansette record player. I was still quite young and only had two small 45rpm records; one was the soundtrack to *Lady and the Tramp* and the other was Bill Haley and His Comets, with 'Rock around the Clock'. The following year, my Dansette was given to my older cousin, Harold.

The radio, or wireless as my parents called it, was on all day long, usually tuned to the BBC Light Programme. Like a lot of families today, we all enjoyed science fiction, so *Journey into Space* was essential listening. This was set in the future of 1965, and starred David Kossoff as Lemmy and Andrew Foulds as Captain Jet Morgan.

I also remember listening to *The Clitheroe Kid* with the tiny Jimmy Clitheroe, who although a grown man, was playing the part of a schoolboy as he was so small. Then there was *Educating Archie* with Peter Brough and his ventriloquist's dummy Archie Andrews, who was always popular with the children of the '50s.

My father used to be a ballroom dancer in his youth, an interest sadly not shared by my mother – fifteen years younger than Dad, she preferred show dance. There was a programme on the radio called *Time for Old Time*, with Sidney Bowman and his orchestra, which played ballroom music, and Dad loved it. Before the programme came on, we pushed the furniture back and rolled up the rugs ready for Dad to teach me the steps to each dance. There wasn't a lot of room, but somehow we managed it. Dad knew exactly how to hold a partner and to guide them through each dance, so I soon learnt the waltz, St Bernard's waltz, the Veleta, a simple quickstep and the Gay Gordons. Whenever we went to a party or function, I would be my father's partner instead of Mum.

There was a great selection of music to listen to on the radio in the 1950s. These are some of the songs I remember listening and singing along to …

There was Sparky and his magic piano. Eve Boswell always seemed to be on the radio singing either 'Sugar Bush', 'Young and Foolish', 'Ready, Willing and Able' and 'Pickin' a Chicken'. Another favourite of mine was '(How Much is) That Doggie in the Window' by Patti Paige.

The radio was ideal for family life, as we could carry on with our hobbies and chores with the radio in the background. This was soon to change when television invaded our home. Instead of talking to each other, we had to be quiet whilst someone was watching a play, comedy or film. Everything changed in the house after that.

TELEVISION

Just before (and because of) the Coronation in 1953, my parents rented a television set from Radio Rentals. The firm had to erect a large aerial in the shape of an H on the roof. The set had a small screen – 12in, I think – and it sat on a table in the corner of the room. It was black and white and there was just one station: the BBC. As we were the first in our immediate family to have a TV, all the relatives who lived close enough came to our house to watch it with us in the evenings, until they had one of their own.

The test card would be on whenever the TV was closed down and a clock came on before each programme. If there was an interval or a breakdown in a programme, a small film of a potter's wheel was shown until the programme was resumed. In the early days, the TV often stopped working and then all you would see would be wavy lines flashing across the screen. Mum then had to go over to the phone box outside the Pelham pub to inform Radio Rentals, who came out straight away to fix it. If it couldn't be mended, the company replaced it with another set.

Some of the programmes my family and I watched were *The Army Game*, a comedy based in an army camp which starred Alfie Bass, Bernard Bresslaw and Charles Hawtrey; *Dixon of Dock Green* with Jack Warner, and *The Larkins*, a comedy sitcom featuring Peggy Mount as loud-mouthed battleaxe Ada Larkin and David Kossoff playing her henpecked husband, Alf. I enjoyed the serials adapted from classic books like *Jane Eyre* (of which there were several in the 1950s), although the music really spooked me. Most people of my age must remember tuning into *The Railway Children*, *David Copperfield* and *Little Women*.

The Quatermass Experiment was a science fiction series starring Reginald Tate as Professor Bernard Quatermass. My mother loved it, but I watched with hands over my eyes, as I found it rather scary; I think it might have been the music. This programme would seem very tame when compared with the modern science fiction today.

I also remember variety shows such as *Sunday Night at the London Palladium* with various compères, but the most popular was of course Bruce Forsyth.

When I was very young, I was glued to the set and *Watch with Mother*, which featured *Picture Book*, *Andy Pandy*, *Bill and Ben* and *Rag, Tag and Bobtail*. My favourite, though, was

The Woodentops. For older children the programmes started at about 5 p.m., but only went on for about an hour and included a children's newsreel. *Crackerjack* was another favourite of mine and compèred by Eamonn Andrews, who had Leslie Crowther and Peter Glaze to accompany him. It was all fun and games, with an occasional performance from a popstar. The last bit of the show was called 'Double or Drop', and all the children contestants had to answer questions. If they got the right answer they won a prize; if they were wrong, it was a cabbage. They had to hold on to all their prizes and not drop any until the end of the quiz.

Once I became a teenager, however, my tastes changed and I became a big fan of the *Six-Five Special*, with Pete Murray as the compère.

four

SCHOOLDAYS

I have conflicting memories of schooldays in 1950s Portsmouth.

I didn't go to a nursery before I started infant school, but I was still looking forward to going, as I didn't know what to expect. So I eagerly entered the reception classroom at the infants' school in Drayton Road, North End, Portsmouth in September 1951, almost three months before my fifth birthday. There wasn't a school uniform, but to start with I wore a navy blue pleated gymslip over a blouse or jumper and also a navy blue gabardine mac in the winter. I also wore a liberty bodice when I was young, which was worn over my vest and had rubber buttons down the front.

As the teacher took my hand and led me away, I didn't notice my mother quickly disappear. The room seemed large and noisy, but was filled with toys to play with. In one corner was a large sandpit with buckets and spades scattered around it. A wooden playhouse was in another corner, with a table, chairs and everything needed to play house. There were dolls and cars and boxes of bricks to play with. On one side of the room were small wooden tables and chairs with paper and crayons to draw on, and Plasticine in various colours to mould into shapes.

The teacher sat at a high desk next to the fireplace, which in winter would have a large coal fire roaring away all day. First thing in the morning, after the teacher checked us against her register, we stood at the front of the room to say our prayers and learn the words to the Lord's Prayer. We were then allowed to play for a while, as we were so young. During the morning a crate of tiny bottles of milk was brought into the classroom and distributed to each child along with a paper straw, which quickly flattened, making it impossible to drink through.

At break time, we were led out into the playground and left to our own devices. The boys ran around yelling and shouting, pretending to be cowboys and Indians, pointing fingers at each other and shouting 'bang-bang'. The girls gathered together in groups of family or friends they knew. I was an only child and didn't know anyone at all, so I stood in the centre of the playground, swaying from side to side, hoping someone would play with me. That first week nobody did, they just ran around me poking out tongues and laughing. I was glad when the bell went and we had to form queues to return to our classrooms.

At dinner time we were taken to the large hall that was also used as a canteen. There were long tables already laid with knives and forks, and we were told where to sit. The meals were delivered to the school in a lorry, with large aluminium containers each with potatoes, vegetables and a meat dish, plus a pudding. This was served to us on a plate and there was no alternative, of course. The dinner lady stood behind us, dressed in a white overall and with a cap on her head. I usually held my knife in my left hand and she made me change. Although I wasn't left-handed, it was obviously frowned upon. I found the food sloppy and bland, and the custard must have been made with water. Before we were allowed to eat, we had to say grace. 'For what we are about to receive may the good Lord make us truly grateful.' I knew the words, as my father said it at home before dinner too.

After that first week, I started going home at lunchtime to a good meal and my family.

The school day started at 9 a.m. and finished at 4 p.m. with a fifteen-minute break morning and afternoon, and ninety minutes for lunch. After the dinner break, the afternoon was spent learning to write our names and drawing pictures. A large rug was on the floor and the teacher sat us all down and read us a story before we all went home.

A few weeks later I was put off school a bit. I had always been taught how to behave and I was too frightened to be naughty, so I was distraught to be wrongly accused of throwing sand into another child's face. The teacher made me stand in front of all the other children, telling everyone what a naughty girl I was. I was very shy and felt humiliated; I really hated the teacher after that episode. On another occasion I asked to visit the toilet, but she refused and made me wait until I went home. This was awful, as I was not yet 5 years old. Another boy was also refused, so he did his business on the floor and she had to clear the smelly mess up. I felt that justice had been done.

I was just beginning to dislike school when a few months later a little girl started. Her name was Margaret Gilkerson, and we became lifelong friends. I was also pleased to have a new teacher, Mrs Tope. I remember her name as she was so lovely to all the children, so I started to enjoy school at last. She had a smiling face with rosy cheeks and curly auburn hair, and everyone wanted to please her. Mrs Tope made learning enjoyable to me and I soon learnt to read, write and count. The first books that I really loved were the *Milly-Molly-Mandy* series. This was a selection of stories about a little girl and her family and friends, and came with a map of her village, showing where everyone lived. The counting was done with the aid of an abacus and bricks.

Jean Palmer, Margaret Gilkerson and Doreen Matthews also went to Drayton Road Infants when they started school.

I remember that at Christmas, the school put on a play for the parents to come and see. One year, I played the part of one of the stars on the tree, dressed in a white dress and covered in tinsel, with another piece round my head. We sang 'Twinkle, Twinkle Little Star'.

Tony Thomas, who would go on to marry my friend Margaret (second from left, back row) at a fancy-dress party at Westover Road School in Copnor, 1950.

Tony Thomas (eighth from right, second row), posing for a photograph at Westover Road School in 1950.

There was another incident that stands out particularly clearly – it seems that health and safety wasn't that widely practised in schools during the '50s. The blackboard was green and stood on a large easel in front of the class. One day, when I was about 7, it fell on my shoulder as I walked past. The teacher sent me straight home, accompanied by another child called Nicholas. I don't recall having any medical attention for this injury from either the school or our doctor. During a medical in my adult years, I was informed that my shoulder had actually broken and reset itself slightly forward with a bump.

When I was 7 years old, at the end of 1953, Margaret and I attended the junior school in Lyndhurst Road, North End, Portsmouth. We had to start serious learning here; all the times tables had to be learnt by heart, and my gran used to test me at home. I was good at reading and spelling and enjoyed English and history, but arithmetic was beyond me, apart from the basics. My poor old mum couldn't help either, as she didn't attend school much as a child in the 1920s.

Granddad had been in the navy, and the family moved around the country a great deal. In fact, at the age of 14, my mother taught herself to read and write with the aid of film books, assisted by her uncle Herby, who also encouraged her to smoke.

I only remember one teacher at this school: Miss Moon, quite a chubby lady with a moon-shaped face, who wore half-moon glasses. She seemed quite elderly, with her grey curly hair and unsmiling whiskery face. She always seemed angry and ready to smack you with a ruler. One day I had put the wrong numbers next to the answers to a mental arithmetic test, so I crossed them out and corrected them. Miss Moon called out my name and told me off. She then pulled up the sleeve of my jumper and hit me hard several times with her ruler on the tender part of my lower arm. She spoilt school for me, so from that point onwards I used any excuse to be off sick and stay at home.

Me knitting (left, front) and my classmates at Lyndhurst Road Junior School, 1956.

I was never picked to be in the school play or Nativity at Christmas, as I was too quiet and shy. Teachers usually chose their favourites, and I was never one of those. I did have a fairly good singing voice, though, so I joined the choir instead, which I enjoyed. We performed in the Copnor Methodist church or at school plays. At Christmas, we children who were in the choir were all dressed as shepherds draped in sheets, with our mums' best tea towels on our heads.

As part of the festive celebrations, a large decorated tree stood grandly in the assembly hall and we all decorated our classrooms. Each of us brought a contribution to our class tea party – sandwiches, small cakes or jellies in paper dishes – and the teacher supplied the orange squash. Any cards we brought for friends were posted in the red cardboard postbox and we all made cards and calendars for our parents with lots of cotton wool and glitter. On the day of the party, we exchanged small gifts with our friends and played a few games.

—

I went to Westover Road School. I could walk there in five minutes, as there were no cars on the road in those days.

Tony Thomas

I think I was in Francis Avenue School, and remember having to walk to the Guildhall swimming baths. We had to walk in a line, with our bathers and towels under our arms in all weathers. One of the teachers was called Mrs Brown and we all had to say good morning to her, and for a joke we called her Mrs Hovis. She was not amused and she made us all stay behind after school as punishment. Also I cannot remember for what reason, but as punishment quite a few of us had to stand on chairs in the assembly hall and our legs were smacked with a ruler. I always remember this as we had huge welts on the backs of our legs which were sore for days afterwards. It can only be for something simple like talking in class, as I was too scared to do anything naughty. Could you imagine that happening today? The teachers would be prosecuted, wouldn't they!

Diane Williams, née LeMettey

I went to Drayton Road Infant School in the '40s and I can remember a large grey barrage balloon used to be let off from the other playground. I went to Lyndhurst Road Junior School and then back to Drayton Road, as the Boys' Senior School was next to the Infant School then.

John Organ

FUN AND GAMES

I remember a few of my contemporaries from junior school; Marilyn Long, Brian Taylor, Brian Lamb, John Smith, David Wright (my cousin), Caroline Pryor and Dorothy Small. There was a Jennifer, Penelope and her friend Heather, but I am afraid I cannot recall their surnames. My group of best friends included June Banks, Jean Bonny, Sandra King, Annette Chipperfield, Jennifer Penwarden, Phyllis Harding and Margaret Gilkerson.

I was also friends with Anne Wooldridge, whose father ran a small ironmonger's shop in Kingston Crescent, Portsmouth. One Christmas, she gave me a small pair of nail scissors in a leather case, purchased from her parents' shop, and they lasted for years. Another girl, Linda Adams, lived in the flat above the Blue Cross animal centre, which was in Commercial Road, Mile End. She took me around the centre, where all the animals were being looked after, and it was sad to see the room where the pets were put to sleep when they were too ill to cure. Linda took me with her to ballroom lessons, which were held in a large upstairs room somewhere in Mile End. Tony Thomas, meanwhile, went to Langstone Road Junior School, which was not far from his first school.

We didn't have mobile phones or iPads to keep us amused, but we did learn imaginative play instead. At break time in school, we played games in the playground such as 'Hey Mr Wolf'. One person stood at the front, with their back to the rest, and the winner was the one who managed to get to him or her without being seen. There was also the potato game. Everyone put their fists forward, whilst another child (the leader) tapped each fist, chanting 'one potato, two potato, three potato, four; five potato, six potato, seven potato, more!' The child whose fist was tapped on 'more' than had to put it behind their back. The winner was the child with their fist still up.

We played various games of chase and skipping games with a long rope, with a child at each end turning the rope. All the other children jumped into the rope and we all sang, 'jelly on the plate, jelly on the plate, and wibble wobble, wibble wobble, jelly on the plate'. The one skipping had to then shake like a jelly without jumping out of the rope. We also played games in a circle such as 'The Farmer wants a Wife'. It was all good fun and there were very few bullies in our schools; it was best to ignore or shout back at them anyway.

Tony (second from right, middle row) at Langstone Road School, Copnor in 1954.

Next to the school was a tuck shop, which was in the front room of a house. For 1d, you could purchase either a packet of broken crisps, a drink which tasted like sugar water with added colouring, or an ice lolly. This was really ice on a stick dipped in fruit drink, which turned to plain ice when you licked it. This was all a bit cheeky, but we all queued up to buy them at the end of the school day, especially if it was warm and sunny.

SCHOOL MEDICALS

Each year we had a visit from the school's medical team, who checked us over. We all stood in line outside the medical room, digging the dirt out from under our nails with hair pins, and combing our fingers through our hair in an effort to appear cleaner than some of us were. We were weighed, heights were noted and the state of our clothes scrutinised. Our bodies, nails and clothes were inspected for cleanliness, neglect and ill treatment, and our hair checked over for nits. Stethoscopes were used to check hearts, and little hammers bumped our knees to see if our reflexes were responding okay. We would then be given an appointment to see the school dentist for a check-up. There would be a note for our parents if we were not up to scratch in the hygiene department.

Mum was obsessive about checking me for fleas and nits. If I scratched my skin at all, she took all my clothes off, searching for any tiny creatures lurking there; before scrutinising the bed with a magnifying glass. If she found any little black vermin, they would be pinched in half until she saw blood. Then everything would be cleaned with Lifeguard disinfectant, Flit sprayed everywhere and we would have to vacate the room. Mum had one of those plastic two-sided combs for checking the hair for nits. Any head scratching resulted in my hair being pulled and carefully combed through; nothing was ever found, thank the Lord. I was terrified of nits in my hair, as Mum sad that all my hair would have to be cut off.

We also had to read the letters on a chart to test our eyes, and I was found to have a squint in my left eye, making it turn in slightly. I had to attend the Portsmouth and South Hants Eye and Ear Hospital. I was sat in front of a machine and had to look through a lens at a picture of a lion and a cage. I had to try to move the handle to get the lion into the cage, and as I couldn't, this meant my eyes didn't work together properly. An operation was suggested – although double vision was a possible side effect – but Mum wasn't keen on this, as she didn't trust hospitals after losing my brother at birth. Instead I had to wear glasses, with a patch of plaster over my good eye to try to get the lazy one to straighten. After a while I didn't bother with the glasses, as I could see okay and my eye only turned when I was tired or upset.

Apart from the usual childhood ailments that most children suffered from in the '50s – mumps, measles, chickenpox, coughs and colds – I was reasonably fit and well throughout my childhood. I did catch impetigo from someone which was rather nasty, but not life threatening. It started as a sore on the back of my neck, close to my hairline and became infected, scabby and weepy. I had to have this purple ointment applied to the infected part and my hair pulled up out of the way. A week or so off school was advised to stop it spreading to other pupils.

There was an outbreak of polio in the 1950s and by 1959, we all had to have the new oral vaccine to protect us. Some of the polio victims had to spend time in what was called an iron lung. This was a large iron machine that the patient lay in to help with breathing difficulties until they (hopefully) felt well again. Some children didn't survive and several were left with a disability.

SCHOOL TRIPS

Unlike the children of today, my friends and I didn't go on long school trips to exciting places.

The only school trip we went on was a daytrip on the Isle of Wight, which we really looked forward to. Every week we had to take in 6d to save towards the day out. We went by coach down to the harbour to catch the Ferry to Ryde, where we carried on to Carisbrooke Castle, our destination. We looked over the castle, had a picnic lunch and bought a few souvenirs before heading back home. I used to collect spoons with place names on the handle, so that was my souvenir for the day out.

We also went to the Kings Theatre in Southsea, to watch the ballet *Swan Lake*. This was the first ballet I had ever seen and I was mesmerised with the splendour of it all.

The school holidays in the 1950s were of a similar length to those nowadays, with two weeks at Easter, one week at Whitsun (now spring bank holiday), six weeks for the summer holiday and three weeks for Christmas. February and October half terms were only two days – Friday and Monday.

SENIOR SCHOOL

At the age of 11 in about January 1957, we all took the 11-plus exam. Those who passed were to go to the Northern Grammar School, which was then in Mayfield Road, North End, or the Southern Grammar School for Boys. Some pupils who passed went to the Portsmouth High School in Southsea, and the rest ended up at secondary moderns. Margaret and I both went to Lyndhurst Road Secondary Modern School for Girls in North End in September 1957, as did Jean Palmer (although she attended seven years before me).

In this school, you were encouraged to try other subjects as well as the academic courses. There was still maths, history, geography, science and English to study. We studied current affairs, but at that time there were no languages to learn.

I remember that the main school had several classrooms, plus a selection of brick-built huts for other subjects. One hut was given over to needlework, with sewing machines, tables for cutting out materials and tailors' dummies to measure correctly. This was a great idea, as this class taught me to make simple clothes for myself, which saved me a lot of money over the next few years. I started off making an apron and in the end I was able to make myself a dress.

Another hut was used as the domestic science room, and it had several small kitchen areas, each with an oven, sink and large wooden table, along with all the equipment needed for cooking. We were divided into small groups to share each area and supplied with an apron and a hat to wear. The first thing the teacher did was to inspect our hands and nails, and our hair had to be short or tied back under the hat. Our first few lessons were about health and hygiene, and we had to bring in a flannel, a brush and comb and a cotton handkerchief. We were then taught to clean the brush and comb, launder the flannel and hanky by hand and how to iron. The teacher told us about various fabrics and how to launder them and what products we could use. There was also a lesson on polishing shoes and another on the correct way to lay a table and a tray for tea.

We had to bring our own ingredients for cooking and something to take it all home in. My handy father made me a large wooden box with a handle in the middle, which had two lids that lifted up. So with my schoolwork in a duffle bag over one shoulder and my food box on the other arm, I soon built up muscles on the walk to and from school.

We were taught how to make short and puff pastry, scones, various cakes and puddings and how to prepare good, wholesome food. The only thing we didn't learn was how to cook a full meal, as I expect it was thought our mothers would do that. I enjoyed this lesson and found it very useful and fulfilling.

Lyndhurst Road School was also an art school, where pupils came from other areas to study art at sixth-form level before applying to Portsmouth Art College. The art teacher was Mrs Welch.

The other teachers I remember were Mrs Vine, who taught history; Mrs Parker, the maths teacher; Miss Smith, a science teacher; and Mrs Leighton, the headmistress.

Margaret and I stayed friends all through school and beyond. We also kept our small group of friends – Jennifer, Phyllis, June, Jean, Sandra and Annette – who we'd known for years.

There were four years in this school, and each year was divided up into grades of ability, Upper and Lower A, Upper and Lower B, Upper and Lower C, and D for the less academic.

Pupils sat facing the teacher, at a desk that they shared with another pupil. The brighter pupils sat in the front seats, on the left-hand side, while the lower-ability students occupied the right-hand seats towards the back. This included me, as I was in the Upper A set, but nearer the bottom of that class. There were forty-six children, and the desks were arranged in four lines. There was no talking allowed in the classroom and everybody learnt to obey the teacher or be punished. This could be just sitting quietly with our hands on our heads, writing lines (for a minor disobedience) or being sent to the headmistress and given a few strokes of the cane across the hand. In extreme cases, the child would be expelled from the school. Luckily I was never in any kind of trouble at school as I lacked confidence in myself then. One girl was expelled for letting off stink bombs in the classroom, and another was very rude to one elderly teacher who was rather easy-going. This girl, who was the daughter of a doctor, used to walk out of her lesson laughing; the poor teacher didn't know how to control her.

I wasn't keen on sports and I hated the swimming lessons. A bus took us to a pool somewhere in Portsmouth near the Guildhall, on what always seemed to be a cold, wet day. The changing rooms were along the edge of the pool, with stable type doors for privacy. The unheated water was freezing cold and there was nowhere to dry our hair, so we went back to school on the bus still wet and cold. I hated indoor pools after that.

We played netball in the playground, and PE was performed in the hall or in the playground when it was a dry day. Whatever the weather, PE was performed in a tee shirt or vest and navy blue knickers with white socks and black plimsolls on our feet. Our school didn't have playing fields, just a hard playground, so if you fell, you ended up bruised or worse. Athletics were practised at Bransbury Park, Milton. Here we ran races, tried the long and high jump and threw beanbags about. The teacher told me that I was a good hurdler, and I then had to practise for the Portsmouth City sports day. This was held each year in Alexander Park, which is now the Mountbatten Centre. I was terrified of having to perform in front of all those people in this large arena, and I had never worn spiked shoes until the day of the event. I completed the race, but I had no idea where I came, as I was so bewildered by it all. Our school won the cup that year and we all had our photo in the *Hampshire Gazette*, but I didn't see the photo as the family didn't buy that newspaper. I don't think I even mentioned the event to my parents as I hated to draw attention to myself.

Everyone in school belonged to a house, the colours of which were red, green, blue or yellow, and this was the colour sash you wore at sporting events. I was in Eversley, which I think was blue, and Margaret was in Netley, which was red. We earned points towards our house for sporting and academic achievements. The teacher also gave us a point for each correct piece of school uniform we wore as well. At the end of the year, the house with the most points won the cup.

We all left school at 15, at Christmas, Easter or summer, unless we were staying on to do the art course. I was considered to be good at art, and Mrs Welch, who taught the subject, suggested that I should stay on another year to study it. If I passed I could have gone to the art college that was near the Guildhall. This was known as Portsmouth College of Art between 1951 and 1961, when it became the City of Portsmouth College of Art until 1965. It was then renamed Portsmouth College of Art and Design until 1994, when it became part of Portsmouth University. I had a boyfriend then who wasn't keen on me joining up with a load of 'Beatniks', as he referred to them, so I didn't stay on and have regretted it ever since.

As far as I remember, we were not offered the opportunity to take any GCEs at secondary school. Some girls retook their 11-plus at 13 if they were bright enough and if they passed, they went on to a grammar school. The rest of us had to practise attending an interview and also had a talk from someone at the local Labour Exchange. Then, armed with our last school report and reference, we were sent on our way out into the big wide world.

—

My last school was Copnor Modern School in Copnor, Portsmouth; to get to that we had to go over what was then called the Stone Bridge, which has now been replaced with a metal one.

Tony Thomas

I went to Northern Grammar School, which was in Mayfield Road then. I enjoyed sports such as tennis, rounders, hockey, netball and table tennis. I loved my schooldays: the studying, playing sports and the camaraderie. One incident I remember – bearing in mind it was the early days of rock and roll – was being caught with some of my friends doing the 'boo-bop-a loola', or in other words, bopping. The teacher was not amused and we all ended up in detention, but it was worth it to see the look on the teacher's face.

Whilst wearing my full grammar school uniform, including the hated brown beret, a boy from another school snatched the beret from my head and posted it into a red postbox. I was pleased to get rid of it at first, then realised I would have to buy a new one, so I stayed next to the postbox until a postman came to empty it. The postman's comment was, 'You really should have put a stamp on this, but I will let you off this time.'

Doreen Matthews, née Linsdale

I went to the Southern Grammar School for boys, both in the old school in Highland Road from 1953 to 1955 and also the new school at Baffins from 1955 to 1958.

I was also in the Boy Scouts, and during my time as a patrol leader, our troop were invited to a Christmas party organised by the Girl Guides. I felt that my chances of making a good impression with one of the girls would be somewhat hampered by arriving in my Scouts uniform of shorts, neckerchief and woggle, so I dashed home and changed into long trousers, a smart shirt and Bill Maynard-type jumper. Upon my return, the scoutmaster admonished me for not looking like a Boy Scout and I was asked to leave the troop, before ever having a chance to net a girl.

Ken Matthews

The school [St Jude's Senior School in Southsea] had a club, which I enjoyed. We played table tennis, snooker and danced.

Diane Williams, née LeMettey

five

FAMILY AND FRIENDS

Most of our fun times in the 1950s included family members and were more important than any material goods we wished to have. Our family were noisy, funny and generous with their time with each other. There was plenty of laughter, a few tears of sadness, of course, when older members started to climb the steps up to Heaven, but what we did have then was each other to try to make life happy again. There was no counselling then, no stranger helping you to find your inner self; you made things better with a cup of tea and a nice long chat with a member of your own family.

Things did start to change when cars were available to the masses, and then everyone felt they should move further away. With more cars on the road, we could no longer play in the street and friendships became more difficult to keep. Television didn't help either, as there was always a programme that couldn't be missed and at family gatherings the television became the focus of attention and people forgot how to chat.

FAMILY HOMES

My family had to share housing and make do in the early part of the 1950s but still enjoyed time spent together. The weekend before and after Dad's week off would be spent visiting Mum's relatives. Housing was in short supply in Portsmouth during the early 1950s, and so was money, so some of the relations moved about to various locations.

My mum's sister May Legg and her husband Harold lived with us for a short while until they moved to a house on the corner of Pink Road and Powerscourt Road in Portsmouth. They lived in that house, along with daughter Iris Delves and

My family making music in Beresford Road in 1955.

her husband Bob and May's youngest child, her son Harold.
Young Harold did his National Service in the RAF and played in
the band there. When they lived at our house, the front room
was full of his musical instruments. There was a saxophone,
clarinet, squeezebox and a beautiful piano accordion in white
pearl. One day, the whole family gathered in our garden with
these instruments, plus Dad's drums, and made one hell of a din.
The neighbours must have been so pleased to have us there.

Iris and Bob – a Londoner – started married life in a flat
in the Guinness Buildings in London. They then spent a short
time at our house before moving in with her parents, May and
Harold Legg. For a while Iris and Bob lived on a houseboat
in Milton Locks, where they had to use a rowing boat to get
back to shore when the tide came in. By the late 1950s they
were living in a static caravan in Milton caravan site, which
was residential then. This caravan had a small kitchen and Iris
washed some of her clothes in a Baby Burco wash boiler.
This machine was also handy if you needed to make several
pots of tea, although Iris also had a Goblin teasmade. Their
double bed folded into the wall and was pulled down at night.
The caravan was warm and cosy and had everything they
needed, especially as they both worked full time in the civil
service. Iris and Bob eventually bought a house of their own
and later owned a shoe shop in Forton Road, Gosport.

THE SHANTY HOME

Later in the 1950s, Auntie May and Uncle Harold moved into
a small wooden house in Milton Locks, Portsmouth, called
'the Shanty'. At the time there was an entire village of these little
homes by the sea; they were once used by fishermen's families.

The Shanty was home to May and Harold Legg in the 1950s. *Front row, left to right:* Iris Delve and Harold, May and Julie Legg.

Although it was small, with only two rooms, my uncle and aunt made it into a cosy home. They built a balcony on the front with a tiny garden full of flowers. The back room was their bedroom, and there was a passageway separating the two rooms. This was used as a kitchen, with a sink at one end for washing dishes and clothes. At the other end was a small Baby Belling electric cooker and cupboards for food and cleaning materials. The front of the house was the living room, which was heated with a cast-iron room heater with a chimney which burnt anthracite. Auntie made the room look so pretty with floral curtains and chair covers, and it always looked inviting. As the Shanty was so close to the sea at Milton Locks, my uncle owned a small rowing boat.

Uncle Harold always had a cigarette on the go and would light up the next ciggie with the last one, so his fingers were dark brown with nicotine stains. He rode a bicycle to and from

The huts in Milton Locks, where my Auntie May and Uncle Harold lived in the 1950s. (*Yesterday Magazine*)

work as a carpenter in Portsmouth Dockyard. The majority of dockyard men rode a bike then, so there were always hundreds of bikes on the roads at the beginning and end of the working day. If you were unfortunate to come to a crossroad as they were all heading home, you had a long wait until they all dispersed.

Opposite the Shanty was the Thatched House pub, and the landlord allowed my aunt and uncle to use their toilet facilities. Uncle Harold, like several of my family members, was a musician and he played the grand piano in the lounge bar of the pub. He used to wear a navy blue dinner suit and black patent shoes. Instead of shirts, he wore a bib-type insert over his vest with a black bow tie. Auntie May worked on the bar serving drinks and keeping the place clean, and sometimes she sang with Uncle Harold on the piano. The Thatched House had a conservatory on the front of the pub facing the sea, and this is where my cousin Diane and I sat with our lemonade and packets of crisps, whilst the rest of the family were drinking in the bar and singing around the piano. Sometimes Diane and I went exploring around the seashore. Once, she got stuck in the mud and had to leave her shoes behind to free herself.

When young Harold married his wife Julie, they lived in Burlington Road in North End. Then, once his parents had moved to Milton Locks, he and his wife lived in a larger wooden house called 'the Meltonia' in Milton Locks. Their first baby, Simon, was born whilst they lived there. In the 1950s our family lived close together and in Portsmouth, so we visited them most weekends, or they came to us. It was lovely to be able to spend so much time together.

Auntie May's other daughter, Joyce, and her husband Roy started married life in a house in Paulsgrove, near Portsmouth, while Roy was away in the RAF. Their daughter Diane was the same age as me, so we were great friends as well as cousins. The journey to visit them in Paulsgrove involved a bus ride, and it was lovely then because it was surrounded by countryside. The house was new, modern, light and airy with large rooms and a long garden.

Roy's parents were publicans in Portsmouth, and so it was inevitable that he would want to run a pub too. The first place he managed with Joyce was the Shearer Arms in Shearer Road, Portsmouth. They made a success of it and soon moved to the Clarendon Tavern, near the Strand in Southsea. It was opposite The Granada Pub, but is no longer a pub; instead it is now a convenience store.

HOLIDAY COMPANIONS

During our summer holiday, Diane and I used to take it in turns to stay in each other's homes for a few days. If it was my turn to stay with her when she lived in the Clarendon Tavern in the Strand, Southsea, we used to take a few sandwiches and spend the day on the beach. Joyce and Roy would sometimes join us in the afternoon as the pubs were all closed then. We didn't use suncream in the 1950s, and one day I was very red and burnt when we went home for our tea. I also felt hot and sick and had a headache, so I suppose I must have had slight sunstroke. I didn't feel like eating that evening and when the sheets touched my tender skin, it felt as though I was on fire. When I returned home, Mum covered me with calamine lotion to soothe it. A few days later my skin peeled off in tiny layers, so I was more careful after that. Some people used to put oil on their skin to go brown; this method must have fried them.

I didn't spend any time in the bar at the Clarendon Tavern when it was open. I only went in there in the morning when it was empty, but it still smelt of stale beer and cigarette smoke from the night before. Diane and I spent the time before bed in their large family room at the back of the pub. This room was heated by a large black cast-iron range, and it was quite cosy in the winter. Diane's father Roy used to put together plastic model vintage cars as a hobby, and they were painted in bright colours and sat on a shelf. Joyce always looked really glamorous behind the bar and wore sparkly tops in the evening. Diane and I were often left to our own devices in the Clarendon Tavern, and one time Diane picked out a cigarette butt from the ashtray that her parents left on the table, as all the family smoked in the '50s. The range was lit, as it was winter, and Diane put a piece of newspaper into the flames to light the butt. Instead, she almost set the rug on fire. Luckily no one found out, or we would have been in real trouble.

When Diane came to my house, we had great fun together. During the day we stored away snacks and sweets for our midnight feast. We sometimes slept in my parents' bed and in the middle of the night woke each other up and ate our treats.

We kidded ourselves that my mum knew nothing about it, but she must have done. My mum was always good fun and made us laugh. She built us tents in the garden, let us make dens under the table when it was raining outside and we were allowed to stay up much later than we should have done. We used to dance and sing and get so excited that we both screamed with laughter, until she warned us that there would be tears before bedtime.

A few years later, Diane and her family moved to Gosport, to a pub called the White Horse Inn in Bridgemary. Although this meant a short trip on the Gosport ferry, we still continued to stay with each other during the summer. This stopped when Uncle Roy was made landlord of the Hayling Billy and the family moved to Hayling Island. Diane and I were teenagers by then and too old for sleepovers.

I spent the rest of my holiday playing with my friend Margaret in either her house or mine, and her mother Ina often took us to the beach, sometimes the one on Hayling Island. To get there you caught a bus down to the small ferry boat that took you across the small stretch of water; I think it cost about 6d per person. Hayling Island was covered in sand and had huge sand dunes to play in. Families used to gather together inside one of the dunes, out of the sea breeze. They laid out their picnics and there was a bit of privacy to change into your beachwear. In the evenings, young lovers used the dunes to do their courting.

There was plenty of room on the beach to play ball games without loads of pebbles hurting your feet. There was a small stall selling ice creams and buckets and spades as well, and towards the ferry was the Ferry Boat Inn pub. My mother always warned me not to pick anything up from the beaches in the '50s, as there might be a remnant left over from when they were used for defence during the Second World War. You also had to beware of broken glass, as some people buried glass bottles in the sand and beaches were not kept so clean.

Margaret, like her mother, Ina, was born in Scotland. Every year, her various Scottish relations arrived in Portsmouth for their annual summer holiday with Ina, her husband Cyril Gilkerson and their family. They took me along on some of their days out too. They all loved South Parade Pier, with its shows and dancing, and also the fair at Clarence Pier. They were a lovely lively bunch to spend time with.

Margaret and I played with dolls until we were about 12 years old, and we also had hula hoops and yo-yos when they came into fashion, as well as a skipping rope, which was always in use. Margaret had a two-wheeled bike, but I wasn't allowed one as my parents worried that I would get injured on the road. I had a two-wheeled scooter but not roller skates, as these too were deemed too dangerous. One day Dad brought home an old bike frame he found in a skip. He cleaned it and fixed it into the grass in our garden in Beresford Road; I loved this and imagined I was cycling around the countryside on it. Although my dad's shed was always full as he used it all the time for making and mending things, Margaret's dad didn't use his shed so it became our playhouse in her garden. We often sat in there and ate jam sandwiches whilst playing house.

KEEPING IN TOUCH

It wasn't easy to keep in touch without a telephone in the 1950s, but we managed somehow.

Our house didn't have a phone and not many people we knew did, apart from Joyce and Roy, as they ran a pub. If Mum wished to use a phone to ring Joyce or report a television fault to Radio Rentals, then she used the public phone in the red box outside the Pelham pub in Chichester Road. There were loads of these lovely red phone boxes in the 1950s and you didn't have to walk far to find one in Portsmouth. The big heavy door closed behind you when you were inside and you could have a private conversation sheltered from the extremes of the weather. Lovers sometimes used them for a quick kiss and cuddle on the way home in the evening. Sometimes a queue formed outside and if you took too long with a call, a loud knock would be heard on one of the small windows and then an angry face glared at you, telling you to hurry up.

The phone was black Bakelite (an early form of plastic, but very hardwearing). There was a chrome dial on the front, and you picked up the receiver from its cradle and inserted two old pennies in the slot. You then dialled the number and when the person answered, you pressed button A. If nobody answered, you pressed button B for your money to be returned. Each phone box had its own telephone number, so you could ask someone to phone you at a certain time and then wait outside for it to ring. My friend Margaret used to wait in the box outside the Pelham, and I went to the other one in Chichester Road outside the Lord Chichester pub and we rang each other. Not having a phone at home, we thought this was great fun. We also phoned the speaking clock, and in 1950, the voice was provided by Ethel Jane Cain, who would tell you the precise time in her eloquent voice. You needed to take a few pennies with you, as sometimes the call you were making would take longer than expected; if the beeps sounded and you ran out of money, you would be cut off. In Portsmouth, the calls were managed by the switchboard in Telephone House, Southsea, and my Auntie Iris worked there as an operator in the 1950s.

Close to the phone box, you could usually find a red letter box too. There were two deliveries of post – one in the morning and another at lunchtime on weekdays. On Saturday, there was just one delivery, and none at all on a Sunday. Stamps could only be purchased from the post office or a stamp vending machine, which was usually located outside the post office. We didn't have first- and second-class stamps then. The postman was dressed in a very smart dark navy suit, with a peaked cap, and usually rode a bike.

Telegrams were in use then, and you ordered these at the main post office in your area. Once the customer had chosen their desired variety, they would write the message on the form provided (as concisely as possible, since the charge was approximately 1s 6d per word). Telegrams could be used for anything, but tended to convey wedding and birthday greetings.

At the back of the main post office was the teleprinting room, which had large metal typewriter-like machines, with spools of white gummed paper coming out of them. The message was printed on this paper, stuck on the required telegram and put into an envelope. This was taken into another room, where the messengers were waiting to deliver them to their destination. If the telegram was destined for another district, it was sent electronically to the delivery office close to that address.

HOME ENTERTAINERS

We had no need to go to the theatre regularly for entertainment. Even at home, Dad would entertain us all, sometimes just by removing his false teeth and gurning at us through his bare gums. For such a handsome man, he could look quite alarming. On one occasion, Mum, Emily and I and maybe other visiting relatives were sitting quietly chatting with a cup of tea, and Dad went off to do something. Much later the doorbell rang and I answered it. Standing at the door was a rather grotesque looking 'lady'. With Mum's old mac around his shoulders and his trousers pulled up to his knees under one of Emily's floral overalls was my father. He had a headscarf tied round his chin, covering what looked suspiciously like one of my mother's new string mop heads. Dad's face was plastered with lipstick smeared across his lips and on both cheeks, with a huge beauty spot pencilled on his chin. 'Is your mother in, dearie?' he enquired with a gummy smile as everyone erupted in laughter around me. As my father was so smart and vain, no one could believe he was prepared to dress up like this just to make us all laugh.

My cousin, Harold Legg, was another joker: after Dad had fallen asleep after switching off his hearing aid, I remember him creeping up to Dad and switching it back on, shouting, 'You alright Jerry, me old mate?' Poor Dad would jump in fright but never be angry. Harold could get away with murder as he was once the baby of the family before Diane and I came along, twelve years after he was born. He pegged my favourite teddy bear on the line one summer and kept hoisting it out of my reach until I screamed, but he was always forgiven.

I come from a musical family that entertained in pubs, clubs and function rooms throughout Portsmouth. My father was also a drummer in a band and he used to lay his drum kit – or jazz band, as he called it – out in the backyard in Arthur Street to do any repairs. The main drum was made of wood and had to be repainted with a new skin, put on when necessary. Dad had five wooden skulls painted red and silver, which were along the top of the drum and brass cymbals that had to be shone till they looked like gold. There was also a small kettle drum that stood on a metal stand. When he put his drums back together, I was allowed to play on them if I was careful.

Whenever there was a family party or wedding, we always had plenty of entertainers to keep us amused. Uncle Harold, Mum and young Harold played the piano, and young Harold had musicians he could call on to make up a band when

Me playing my dad's drums in the yard at Arthur Street in 1949.

required. My mother had a strong, powerful, magnificent voice and could mimic Sophie Tucker to perfection, so always sang 'Some of These Days' with so much emotion we were all frightened she would collapse with the effort. Al Jolson was another favourite and sometimes at family gatherings she blackened her face with greasepaint and put on a curly wig, blazer and trousers, performing a selection of his songs. If she sang 'Sonny Boy', then my Uncle Roy LeMetty would pull up his trouser legs, put a scarf round his head and sit on her knee with his thumb in his mouth while she sang to him. On another occasion my mother wore trousers and wellington boots with a red cape over her head and shoulders like a sheik and sang songs from the film 'Desert Song'. Her favourite song was 'One Alone'.

While Mum was singing, Dad would have been dancing round the room dressed up in a long dress and hideous make-up with a long wig made of sisal rope, looking like he had escaped from the pantomime. Sometimes Mum and Dad dressed up as Laurel and Hardy and did a little dance skit, singing the duo's theme song or 'On the Blue Ridge Mountain of Virginia'. Dad also used to borrow one of Gran's fur coats and team up with Bob Delves, performing as Flanagan and Allen 'Underneath the Arches'.

CARROLL LEVIS DISCOVERY SHOW

Young Harold had a friend called Gordon, who was also a musician, and they put an act together. Carroll Levis was a Canadian talent scout in the 1950s and he staged the 'Carroll Levis Discovery Show', introducing young musicians and variety acts. Harold and Gordon were one of his discoveries, and we all went to see them. They performed on various instruments, as well as less traditional items, such as a scrubbing board and a saw used like a violin, and they were very good. Harold gave this up when he married and had a family, but continued playing the piano or organ. He performed in clubs and at functions in the evenings and weekends in and around Portsmouth and Hayling Island.

GREAT ENTERTAINERS

My parents played in several pubs over the years and of course I could not accompany them as a child because of the licencing laws. Most of the pubs they performed in are no longer there. The Mediterranean in Stamshaw, Portsmouth, has now been turned into a house. The Oakwood pub, which was in Northern Parade and closed in 2009, is now a Co-operative store and the Royal Dragoon, situated in Kingston Crescent until 1970, is an office block. I remember them playing in the Derby Tavern, still trading in Stamshaw; the Northsea Arms, in Twyford Avenue until 1981; and the Salutation (operating in New Road until 2012). The Beresford pub, which is now flats, and The Lord Roberts were both in Twyford Avenue, where the flyover was later built.

I sometimes accompanied my parents when they were entertaining at an event. While I sat on a chair with a glass of lemonade and a packet of crisps, Dad would be banging away on his drum kit with a huge grin on his face. Sometimes he blew on a metal bazooka to accompany the tune. He had a large suitcase with a few dressing up togs to make people laugh: hats, funny glasses and moustaches, and wigs that he made out of sisal rope. Dad also painted a nude lady on one side of his kettle drum and he used to tickle this with one of his metal brush sticks, making the men giggle as the brush caressed the private parts of her body. Inside the case were also different sized bazookas, a tambourine and a pair of red maracas, plus anything else to make a noise with that he had collected over the years.

Mum had never had a piano lesson in her life; she couldn't read music and so played everything by ear. At home, she used to listen to a song on the radio and then keep practising on the old upright piano in the front room until she perfected it to the best of her ability. She kept a small notebook with her which contained the names of all the songs she knew by heart, along with any fiddly bits jotted down to remind her how it went. She collected sheet music but only for the words; the notes meant nothing to her.

In 1959, she bought me a Grundig tape recorder for Christmas, to make up for giving my record player to her nephew, young Harold. This was a grey machine that externally, looked very similar to a record player. Inside were two spools, with brown tape running from one spool to the other. There were small round brass buttons in the front to press to record, rewind, pause and play, and switches for the volume and bass control. A round grey microphone stood on a small base; this plugged into the tape recorder to sing or talk into and record. Although it was bought for me, Mum loved using this machine as she could record a song from the radio, practise the tune on the piano and play it all back to see if it sounded okay. She could also record programmes from the radio or TV to listen to later, although of course this was only a soundtrack. The video recorder was not available until much later, in the 1970s. We had tremendous fun with my tape recorder, especially at family parties. I used it to record my favourite pop songs and if you wrote down the number it was recorded on you could find it later. I had several tapes filled with music, just like a collection of records. The difficult part was catching the song in between the DJ presenting it and the start of the song. I mainly recorded songs from Radio Luxemburg, although there was a lot of interference and interruptions from advertising, but it didn't bother me too much.

When my parents entertained at weddings or parties, which they did often between 1950 and 1966, there was always someone who wanted a song she had not heard before, so she then had to say, 'You sing it and I will try and play it.' Somehow she struggled through, but the worse bit for her was whenever some drunken wannabe singer stood by the piano literally shouting and screaming through a song, and Mum had to try and keep up with them, her head aching with the din. She couldn't refuse as the so-called singer was usually the father of the bride or groom. Although his voice was awful, the rest of the party group – who were by now very merry with drink – used to cheer him on and put in more requests. This delighted the 'singer', who obviously thought he was destined for fame one day and he continued until he was hoarse and my poor mum was going demented and deaf. It didn't bother Dad as he would have switched his hearing aid off by this point.

I, meanwhile, would be sitting staring at my feet, reading a comic or book or people watching. At the beginning of the evening everyone would be talking quietly, maybe having a little waltz around the dance floor, eating some food and sipping a drink. As the evening grew later and more drinks were consumed, the talking became louder with some shouting across the room at one another. The dancing became a little crazy and fast and instead of sedate steps, legs would fling in the air doing the Gay Gordons, the swing, cha cha, the Lindy Hop (I think this was similar to a jive) or the jitterbug, which was very fast. There was also a dance then called the stroll, in which everyone formed two lines facing one another; women on one side, and men on the other. The couple at the end joined hands and did a fancy step down the line to the end, followed by another couple with a different dance move.

As the evening went on, everyone would want a sing-song. As it was so soon after the war, some of the songs from that era were often requested by the older members of the party. Several people would gather round the piano and loud melodic voices would belt out the old favourites such as 'The White Cliffs of Dover' and 'Pack up your Troubles in your Old Kit-Bag'. There were a few modern ones added by the younger members, and some tears shed by people remembering the loved ones they had lost in the war years. Old married couples sang love songs to one another such as 'My Old Dutch', and 'If you were the Only Girl in the World'. As it was Portsmouth, there would always be a rendition of 'All the Nice Girls Love a Sailor' and 'I Do Like to be Beside the Seaside'.

The only downside for me at these parties and functions was the smoke. We didn't have air conditioning and so the windows had to be flung open, but it was still awful for a child. By the end of the evening, when some of the guests were past caring, several cigarette butts would be stamped out underfoot on the wooden floor. Being very small, I seemed to be surrounded by butts, old discarded bits of food and empty bottles and glasses with beer dregs in, some with cigarette butts and ash floating in the top.

Late in the evening, the guests would form a ring on the dance floor, performing the Hokey Cokey and sometimes the conga around the room. Then there was a last waltz of some sort and also the song, 'Now is the Hour that We Must Say Goodbye'. This song was very appropriate for Portsmouth, with its large sailor population going off for long stints at sea. Some sailors were away for two years or more in the 1950s.

As the bar staff collected glasses and plates and swept up the dog ends and rubbish off the dance floor, Mum and Dad would pack up the drum set for the journey home in the taxi. Everything was wrapped and packed carefully away, as this was my father's pride and joy (after Mum and me). There were the brass cymbals, various drumsticks and the red and silver wooden skulls; the kettle drums and stands and the base drum with its rubber striker on a pedal that Dad thumped with his foot in time with the music. At the front of the drum, facing the audience, was a wooden carving of a boy with a bugle painted blue. This was all packed into the case and large leather carrying case that Dad had made for it all.

The best part of the evening for me was hearing the taxi driver call out the magic words 'Taxi for Vi and Jerry' through the mike. Soon the refreshingly cold night air hit, and I would fall asleep in Dad's arms in the back of the taxi. I don't remember arriving home or being put to bed.

THE BUFFALOES

Dad was also a member of the Royal Antediluvian Order of Buffaloes, a secret society for men which was similar to the Freemasons, I think. The club did a lot of work for charity. He attended the meetings regularly for years, from before he

Buffalo comrades Fred Urry on the drums, Harold Legg Senior on piano, Harold Legg Junior on accordion and his friend Gordon on guitar in Oddfellows Hall in the 1950s.

met my mother until 1955, and several male members of my family belonged to the club too. The lodge was called Manor Lodge, according to the inscription on the back of one of his medals. I think they used to meet in a clubroom in Kingston Crescent, possibly Oddfellows Hall, although I am not sure about that. Dad never told us what went on at the meetings; all we knew was that he had a secret password to use to get in. He never revealed this to us. I think most of the members were involved in the world of entertainment, and they helped one another and local charities in times of need or hardship.

At some of the functions the Buffaloes ran for charity, my mother accompanied Dad on the piano and I went along too. These must have been at Christmas, as there was a real party atmosphere, with singing and dancing and cabaret acts. Dad would do a little drum roll to announce the entertainer for that evening. I remember one magic act, where the man picked coal out of a bucket by the fire and crunched it with his teeth, looking like he was enjoying a tasty meal. He then unscrewed a glass electric light bulb and took bites out of this without cutting his mouth, and everyone was amazed. There was dancing, mainly old-time ballroom, and if another band was playing as well, then Dad and I would have a little dance around the dance floor, with him holding me gently and whispering the steps and 'one, two, three' in my ear. At the end of each dance Dad always twirled me round and bowed, while I curtsied and then he kissed my hand. Dad never had a shortage of dance partners; he was very popular as he danced so well. Mum sometimes became a bit jealous and agreed to do a slow shuffle round the floor with him, but she really hated it.

There were several men with chains of office hanging round their necks, accompanied by their wives. A Master of Ceremonies did all the announcements and arranged a raffle, with all the cash raised that evening going to the society's chosen charities. There would have been a list pinned up of all the other special events going on that year, such as coach outings, children's parties and charitable evenings such as auctions. Most of these events took place between 1950 and 1954, as far as I can remember.

In the summer we went on coach trips with the Buffaloes to places of interest, such as the New Forest or Bournemouth. We even took a trip to Stonehenge, which was more interesting then as you could walk around the enormous stones and take photos and you didn't have to pay for the privilege in those days. Rowland's Castle – a village on the border between Hampshire and Sussex – was a popular choice as well. The castle was destroyed in the fifteenth century, but there were some parts of its walls left when we went there. The coach trip, of course, had several stops on the way at pubs and cafés for refreshment. When we arrived at our destination, there would sometimes be a meal laid on for us all in a hall. I remember a trip to the New Forest, and in the hall close by there were long tables laid out with lily-white tablecloths, cutlery and condiments, ready for our meal. We were given a small bowl of soup, with a bread roll and butter. After that, ham salad with boiled potatoes were served and to follow, there was jelly and fruit. Also on the table were plates of white thinly sliced bread and butter, with dishes of jam and pots of tea to finish.

Dad knew all the men on the trips and we usually paired up with his friend – who I think was called Harry Hawkins – and his wife. Harry worked in a funeral parlour in Kingston Road, Portsmouth. I think it was called Staplefords, and he and his family lived above the shop. He used to sing a funny song at functions and parties called 'I'm Not All There, There's Something Missing'. His daughter – Veronica, I think was her name – was a few years older than me, but we enjoyed each other's company on these outings, parties and social gatherings. Veronica, being the eldest, looked after me and accompanied me on the rides if there were any.

On the way home, my parents and I chose the back seat so I could have a nap. There were usually crates of beer and lemonade on board, which were swiftly consumed by all. Of course this resulted in a sing-song with songs such as 'Show Me the Way to Go Home'.

The air in the coach was smoky and smelt of beer, so a few windows would be opened. Soon most of the happy throng were sleeping, with just a few still singing softly. I was rocked to sleep with the motion of the coach, which I found comforting, only to be awoken by the driver now and again shouting out destinations: 'Who's for Hilsea?', 'We are at Mile End' or 'It's Fratton Road next, ladies and gentlemen!' Then each group of passengers would leave their seats calling goodbye and waving to everyone. By the time North End was announced I was being carried off by Dad, home to my nice warm bed.

BRIDESMAIDS

I had the pleasure of serving as bridesmaid on several occasions. The first wedding was that of Cousin Harold and Julie, and it was at the Register Office in Portsmouth. Diane and I weren't proper bridesmaids, but we had new dresses for the day and wore headbands with silk flowers. My dress was knee length and white, with lemon silk thread going through it. It was really pretty and became my party frock that year.

When we were 12 years old, Diane and I were bridesmaids to our cousin Jean Organ when she married David Palmer. The dresses were made by a local dressmaker in floor-length white satin, with a white net overskirt and puffed sleeves. We wore nylon gloves and floral headdresses and carried a posy. The wedding was in St Michael's Catholic Church in Gladys Avenue. For some reason, whenever there was a wedding in the family, my mother chose to have my poker-straight hair permed at the local hairdressers. This was quite a frightening experience for a child in those days. It involved some obnoxious-smelling lotion plastered on the hair and these large hot electric clip things on wires attached to the hair, burning it into shape. You could smell the hair being singed and I ended up with a frizzball of a style. Lovely!

Me acting as bridesmaid for Jean and David Palmer. I am pictured with my mother and father at St Michael's Catholic church in Gladys Avenue, Portsmouth in 1959.

Jean Palmer, née Organ, at her wedding to David in St Michael's Catholic church, Portsmouth in 1959.

—

Portsmouth was starting to come to life again after the war although the food was still on ration. I was young and we enjoyed ourselves and all played together.

Jean Palmer, née Organ

My dad was in the navy, in the Fleet Arm, and his dad worked in the dockyard in the '50s. They both used to go over to the Jolly Taxpayer pub across the road in Eastbourne Road, Portsmouth. I remember sitting outside on the step of the pub, waiting for Granddad whilst he went into the Bottle and Jug to buy his beer to take home. There were over 1,000 pubs in Portsmouth in those days; now there are only about 100 left.

Tony Thomas

six

HOLIDAYS

My father didn't have much time away from working in Portsmouth Dockyard, apart from a few bank holiday long weekends and a couple of days off at Christmas. I remember that he only took one week off as his summer holiday, and that was in August.

EASTER

On Good Friday everything would be closed for the day; only the cinema was open, showing films about the true meaning of Easter. I think the baker and fresh fish shop opened in the morning only. We always had white poached fish with mashed potatoes and peas on Good Friday, and Dad had a piece of salt fish.

Breakfast was always boiled eggs, usually in a new chicken-shaped egg cup. The egg might have a face painted on it, and a pile of bread soldiers for dipping, which is still my favourite treat. There was a large pile of fresh hot cross buns, heated in the oven and smothered with melting butter. We used to sing the song …

Hot cross buns, hot cross buns
One a penny, two a penny, hot cross buns
If you have no daughter, give them to your sons
One a penny, two a penny, hot cross buns.

The rest of the day was spent quietly; although Dad believed in God and used to attend church when he was younger, we didn't go as a family. Mum believed in God but not in the Church, especially when she was refused a church wedding because my dad was divorced. My father taught me to pray and I had a Bible and prayer book. I also attended Sunday school at London Road Baptist Church in North End. I was very young but went on my own as none of my friends went there. The young teacher told stories from the children's Bible and we were given little picture cards of the story. I stopped going when I had to go up to the adult service, which I found so boring that I fell asleep.

After Good Friday the shops were open again on Saturday, but closed for Easter Sunday and Monday, which made a good break for most people, except those in the hospitality industry and the emergency services, of course. For us, this weekend was spent in the company of Mum's relations, usually at our house. Diane and I – being the only children in our family group – would be given several chocolate Easter eggs. It always seemed to be sunny as I sorted out my chocolate collection. All the small chocolates in the larger eggs were put together in a box to be eaten later; I was very careful with my sweets. Occasionally eggs would come with a basket, which I would keep so I could use it to play shops with. One Easter, my parents gave me a cardboard egg with a silver plastic bracelet inside.

SUMMER HOLIDAYS

My family couldn't afford to go away for the holidays, but it didn't matter if you lived in Portsmouth, as there was so much to see and do in a seaside resort.

Dad's week off in August was spent visiting family members and having days out, with one day spent at our local beach in Southsea. Mum would be wearing a cotton summer dress with buttons all down the front and white peep-toe canvas shoes and Dad would be dressed in his suit, with a white shirt and tie and leather shoes. I usually wore a cotton sundress with matching bolero, and white sandals on my feet. Dangling from my hand would be a new brightly painted bucket and spade from Woolworths. Mum carried a large shopping bag containing a towel and my pink woollen two-piece swimsuit that an aunt had knitted for me, plus cardigans for when it turned cold. Dad carried the other bag, packed with a picnic lunch, consisting of cheese and tomato sandwiches, some fruit and a flask of tea. He would also have put in a newspaper or paperback cowboy book to read on the beach, along with his glasses.

To get to Southsea beach we caught a green Southdown double-decker bus. We sat on the front seat upstairs, so I could look all around, out the large windows. Mum could also smoke a cigarette on the way, as it wasn't allowed downstairs. On arrival at the beach, Dad hired a couple of wooden deckchairs for Mum and himself and I sat on my towel or paddled in the sea. The beach was mainly pebbles, but when the tide was out, there was a small bit of sand to make sandcastles. My parents didn't swim, so stayed on the beach fully clothed, although Dad sometimes removed his shoes and socks and rolled up his trousers, exposing his lily-white legs before joining me in a paddle. I always wore a cotton sun bonnet if the sun was hot and Dad would put a knotted hanky on his head if he forgot his straw hat. My woollen bikini was useless if it got wet as it hung down heavy with water, so I also had a cotton ruched bathing suit in mixed colours to wear instead.

After we had refreshed ourselves with the picnic lunch, I put my clothes back on and we all walked towards South Parade pier. The pier was built in 1879, but burnt down in 1904. It was rebuilt in 1908, then unfortunately burnt down again in 1974. The modern version is therefore rather different to the original. There used to be a roller skating rink there, which was also used for beauty contests in the 1950s. A section of the pier was removed during the Second World War, as there were fears that it could be used by an invading German force. To get onto the pier itself, you had to pay 6d to be let through the turnstiles. There was an arcade with penny slot machines; these were just for fun, not to win large cash prizes. One machine had a sailor dummy behind the glass cabinet and if you put your penny in, he started to move and laugh out loud. Everyone standing around this machine couldn't help laughing along with him. There was a machine with ghosts moving about in a small house scene and another with a large gypsy face ready to tell your fortune. A large football hung off another piece of equipment to test your strength and Dad couldn't resist having a punch at this, as he used to box when he was in the army. My favourite was the one that printed your name on a piece of tin when you punched the letters in.

There used to be shows on the pier and I remember sitting on the chairs, licking an ice cream cone, watching a performance by Poirette clowns. There was always plenty to see and do on the pier; fishing, watching the boats sail by and the open air shows. In the evenings, there were famous stars appearing in various summer shows in the theatre on the pier. In 1953 Peter Sellers starred in 'Showtime' and Arthur English and Eddie Grey appeared in 'Ring out the Bells'. In 1954, Reginald Dixon, the organist, was in a show called 'Jump for Joy'. There was also dancing in the open air under twinkling coloured lights at the end of the pier, weather permitting. There were various competitions to enter, such as the 'Miss Southsea Beauty Pageant' – some young girls may even have become famous because of these.

Sometimes we would instead go to Clarence Pier, where a fairground was built in the late 1950s. The only ride I could go on was the galloping horses or the small roundabouts, but we couldn't afford to go there often.

Clarence Esplanade was built by convict labour in 1848, and the pier opened in 1861. Both are named after Lord FitzClarence

Clarence Pier, with the fairground in the background, in the late 1950s. (*Yesterday Magazine*)

who was once Military Governor of Portsmouth. In the beginning, there were freak shows along the side, featuring animals with extra legs, for instance, which was horrible.

Not far from Clarence Pier there was the Rock Gardens; this was so pretty at night, with lots of coloured lights dotted about in the rocks, waterfalls and flowers, and it looked like a magical wonderland to me.

My mother's favourite place in Southsea was the model village, which was wonderful then, especially for a young child, with all the miniature houses and villages to walk through. Happily, it survives to this day. Close by is the Canoe Lake, where you could hire a boat or sail a model one of your own. There used to be a play area for small children, which my cousin Diane and I loved. For 6d each, children could then play on any of the sit-and-ride toys: trikes, cars tractors and horses. We found this great fun, especially if you didn't have toys like that at home. There was a miniature train that used to take children and adults on a small journey within Southsea, which even the adults enjoyed.

On the large Southsea Common you could play ball games or fly a kite if it was a windy day. The common survived as it was necessary for the harbour defences to have a clear line of sight out to sea in case enemy ships approached. In the '50s, the common was used for various open air shows, as well as the circus, when it came to town.

I think it was Billy Smart's, but it could have been several different circuses. I didn't really enjoy this form of entertainment and felt very nervous walking along the planks of wood to my seat and seeing the grass a long way beneath me. I had been frightened by a clown when I was much younger, so they were not my favourites either. There used to be a person dressed in a gorilla outfit that ran into the audience, picked someone up, threw them over his shoulder and ran off with them. As a small child I didn't know this was a man and part of the act, so I was absolutely terrified that he would come after me. The idea of animals preforming certainly didn't appeal to me either. My days as part of the audience in the circus ring were soon cut short when a trapeze collapsed and fell and the acrobat died. I didn't wish to go again.

By the end of a long sunny day, with all the fresh sea air making us tired and hungry, we often had a special treat of a fish and chip supper with mushy peas. We could buy this from any number of stalls close to the beach and then sit on a bench and eat it straight from the newspaper wrapping, smothered with salt and vinegar, washed down with a cup of tea. We sometimes ended our day in a pub with a garden; I think it might have been called the White Horse, near the common. Dad would have a pint of mild and Mum a bottle of Forrest Brown ale. For me it would be a glass of lemonade and a packet of Smiths crisps with the tiny blue screwed-up bag of salt at the bottom.

Dad's special treat was to go over to the Isle of Wight on the ferry. We all dressed in our best clothes, with Dad in his blazer and casual trousers. He loved the journey and it was like a cruise to us, even though it was only about forty minutes long each way. When we arrived in Ryde, we took the train to Shanklin, with its sandy beach ideal for building sandcastles. By taking the lift you ended up at the top of the cliff overlooking the sea, and this is where we ate our picnic lunch on the grass.

Mum always took her Box Brownie camera on our days out, the one you had to look down into to take the photo. We had some good photos taken on that, even though the snaps were

Me and my dad outside a hotel on the Isle of Wight, pretending that we were staying there, in the late 1950s.

only about 2in square. One day, Dad and I posed outside a posh hotel and pretended we had stayed there. This was just a dream, as we could never afford even one night in a hotel in those days.

My mother's special day out was always London as she loved the city; her father was a Londoner, and Dad was born there too. This would mean a train ride from the main Portsmouth and Southsea station, close to Commercial Road. This was an adventure in itself for me. We always took in all the usual sights: Big Ben, Buckingham Palace and Trafalgar Square, where Dad liked to feed the many pigeons (of course, you are not allowed to do that now).

Mum would always book a day out on a coach trip at the Southdown Coach office in North End. We usually ended up at another seaside resort, such as Bognor, Brighton or Bournemouth, or maybe the New Forest. Sometimes it was a mystery trip and we enjoyed them all.

There was also Hilsea Lido in Portsmouth, where I could use the outside swimming pool; this was ideal for splashing about in if the weather was fine. I think it was only about 6d for a child to use the pool. The Lido – or Hilsea Lagoon as it has sometimes been called –was built round the old moat at Hilsea as a major leisure complex throughout the 1930s. It was originally named Hilsea Bastion Gardens in 1934. There used to be tennis courts, a putting green and roller skating rink, and the area was floodlit, which allowed for outdoor dances and late swimming in the pool until 10 p.m. There was also a boating lake where you could hire a rowboat; this had a bridge going across to the other side. If you felt energetic you could walk from Hilsea along the seashore towards Alexander Park, where there was a children's playground with swings, slides and a roundabout.

Sometimes, if we wanted a relaxing day, we could take a picnic to Baffins Pond in Portsmouth and sit on the grass by the water, watching the ducks and swans and throw any spare bread at them.

TRANSPORT

Neither Mum nor Dad could drive and, even if they did learn, could not afford to buy a car. For short distances in and around Portsmouth, we walked or took the bus; it would be the train or coach to go on a day trip. If we were coming home late from a family party or Joyce and Roy's pub, Mum ordered a cab from the Strand taxi firm. It was always the Strand taxi firm, as Mum trusted the company and their drivers were always reliable. Even if they were busy and didn't have one available, she only had to tell them her surname and they suddenly found one for her. As she was such a valued customer, I expect somebody was raised from their slumber.

The main means of transport for us was, of course, the bus. We had the green double decker Southdown buses that operated out of their large depot at Hilsea. I think these buses were for longer journeys outside the city centre. For journeys within Portsmouth, we used the red and white double decker Portsmouth Corporation buses supplied by the council. In the 1950s some of these were trolleybuses, and the city skyline was covered in wires crossing over one another, taking the buses to various destinations. Trolleybuses operated in Portsmouth from 1934 until 1963. Every bus had its own driver and conductor, both dressed in smart black suits and peaked caps. The conductor used to help the elderly, infirm and mothers with children and pushchairs on and off the bus. They would come to your seat and collect the fare by issuing a paper ticket from a metal machine hanging across their body, with a leather bag over the other shoulder to hold the cash. The cost would depend on the length of the journey, but was only a few old pennies within the city. You boarded and left the bus on the wooden platform at the back of the bus with a long handle to pull yourself on to it. In front of you would be a winding staircase to the top deck, where smoking was allowed. Turning to your left took you to the lower deck, where you could also stand if all the seats were taken. There were several double seats and also two longer bench seats facing either side of the aisle as you entered. When the bus was about to stop, the conductor rang a bell to alert the driver and called out the destination reached. He then rang it again before the bus started off again. He or she could give you information about the journey and the number bus you needed and when to get off. They usually had a little chat to anyone willing to listen, which made the trip friendly. Everyone felt safer travelling in the evening with the conductor on board to keep unruly passengers in check.

—

My mum's family from Edinburgh came to stay every summer and sometimes we had holidays in Scotland. I remember going on coach trips with Sainsbury's, as Mum worked for them in Portsmouth when the store was in Edinburgh Road. My family also went to the horse racing.

Margaret Thomas, née Gilkerson

There was Milton Locks, with the houseboats by the shore. The family played football in the mud. When we went over

Margaret Gilkerson (front left) with her parents, Ina and Cyril, and their
Scottish relations.

to Gosport from Portsmouth Harbour, you could watch all the children called mud larks, diving in the mud to search for money that people threw to them. They were covered from head to foot in thick, sticky mud. We went blackberry picking and swimming at Hilsea Lido and the Guildhall swimming baths. There were trips to the Kings Theatre to watch the Pantomime or wrestling.

I also remember Sunday teas at my grandparents' house in Pink Road, near Powerscourt Road with the family, eating winkles and sticking the black spot from the winkle on our faces, with lovely jelly for afters. Corona drinks, all flavours, [were] delivered to your door with the deposit paid on the bottle. If the bottle was returned, I would get thruppence back to spend on sweets.

Diane Williams, née LeMettey

I met my precious wife Doreen at the Young Conservative Youth Club in Kingston Crescent, Portsmouth, on Valentine's Day 1958. Doreen and I became engaged in 1959 and we planned a holiday in Rochester, Kent, with an aunt of mine. In those far-off days we were required by Doreen's father Frank to provide a letter from my aunt enclosing a map of the locations of the sleeping quarters. This we dutifully provided and Frank was happy knowing that my aunt's bedroom would be between mine and Doreen's, providing no opportunity to see each other between bedtime and reveille. How times have changed!

I used to sell chocolate and peanuts at Fratton Park football ground in 1953–54. If I sold two trays at £10 each, then I was paid £2. The attendance at the match was 40,000 in those days.

Ken Matthews

Doreen Matthews, née Linsdale, and her husband Ken at the fair in Southsea, 1958.

[Portsmouth] was a wonderful place to live. People were friendly and always ready to help each other and you felt safe. Children made their own entertainment. When a horse and cart came round the road, the neighbours would all dash out with a shovel in their hands to scoop up the horse dung to put on their roses.

As a family, we enjoyed lots of caravan holidays to various destinations. This was always great fun, especially when twelve of us took a holiday to Lancing in Sussex. On one of the days we decided to see how many of us could ride two bicycles made for four and managed to get eleven on board, as the photo enclosed will show. Needless to say, we didn't get very far, but it was all a good laugh.

Doreen Matthews, née Linsdale, with her family, sharing two bicycles meant for eight, around 1953.

Another time, I spent a holiday with an aunt in Romford, along with my cousins. On one occasion I took off to the park with their dog, with strict instructions to not let him off the lead. Unfortunately, once in the park, he slipped the lead and ran off. I spent the next three hours searching for him and eventually went home to find him sitting there, where he had been for the past two hours. My aunt had search parties out looking for me, so you can imagine what I thought about that dog!

On holiday with my boyfriend Ken in 1958, we visited Brighton by train and went to the beach. We were swimming and sunbathing and somehow lost our return train ticket for home. We then set about digging up a large part of the beach until we eventually found it. What a relief that was!

Doreen Matthews, née Linsdale

seven

SPECIAL OCCASIONS

CELEBRATING THE CORONATION

I was 6 years old when the whole country celebrated the Coronation of Queen Elizabeth II on 2 June 1953.

At Drayton Road Infant School, we were all requested to wear something red, white and blue, so I wore a white dress with a red, white and blue sash and headdress. All the children had to march round the school playground behind an older girl dressed as Britannia, who was riding in a silver carriage made of cardboard. We were all presented with a blue and silver book about the queen. It was called *Elizabeth our Queen* by Richard Dimbleby, and I still have it in my bookcase.

On the day of the Coronation, it was raining in London and all the family watched the procession on our television. There were parties in all the streets and music and dancing, and our family came to our house to celebrate. My cousin Diane arrived, looking very pretty as usual, with a new dress and a flowered garland across her shoulder. She had a tiara perched

Portsmouth Dockyard, decorated for the Coronation of Queen Elizabeth II in 1953. (*Yesterday Magazine*)

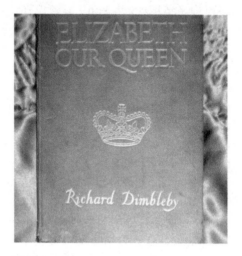

The Coronation souvenir book that was presented to the children of Portsmouth, 1953.

My family outside Beresford Road on Coronation Day, 1953. *From left to right:* Bob Delves, Joyce LeMettey, May and Harold Legg, Fred Urry, Iris Delves and Roy LeMettey.

on her plaited hair, while I had a large silver crown. In our family photo, she looks perfect, and I am next to her, looking awkward, with crossed knees and the crown over one eye. As a memento, I was given a small painted Coronation coach and horses made of tin.

—

My cousin Diane (left) and me (right) outside Beresford Road on Coronation Day.

We had a street party in Havant Road, but Mum and Dad went up to London to watch the Coronation. My brother John and I stayed at home for the party, and our Auntie Ethel looked after us. I entered the fancy dress competition as a Coronation scrapbook and won.

Jean Palmer, née Organ

I remember the street party in Balfour Road: all the tables laid out in red, white and blue. Also the fancy dress, and I wore a red, white and blue dress.

Margaret Thomas, née Gilkerson

Margaret Gilkerson (left) and me (right) in our school Coronation outfits.

All the families got together and had a Coronation street party in Chesterfield Road, Portsmouth. Out came all their tables and chairs into the middle of the road and filled with food and cakes. The Guildhall was decorated with flags and bunting and we caught the trolleybus down to the city centre to see it all.

Tony Thomas

Tony Thomas (far left, front) at a neighbour's Coronation street party in Chesterfield Road, Copnor, in 1953.

We watched the Coronation on the black and white television in our house in Balfour Road. My grandfather, who I called Gan Gan, sent away for two Coronation books and I still have them today.

Doreen Matthews, née Linsdale

Our street, Newcomen Road, held a party for all the kids and we watched the Coronation on the black and white TV bought specially for the occasion.

Ken Matthews

BONFIRE NIGHT

Our family didn't celebrate Halloween in the 1950s and I don't remember anybody who did, as this was seen as an American celebration. But we did have fun on Bonfire Night. The streets of Portsmouth were filled with children with a guy in a cart or old pram, calling out 'Penny for the Guy please', whilst holding out a cap or bucket for money. Some of the guys were just a pile of rags, but others were rather good and some children dressed up a younger brother and stuck him in the cart with a mask on.

I wasn't allowed on the streets to beg for money, but I always had a guy. Mum and I started to make our guy about a week or so early, after we had collected enough newspaper for his body. There always seemed to be an old pair of Dad's trousers and a shirt or jumper that was too tatty for him to wear. We filled this with paper, tying string at the end of each sleeve and trouser end. We then made a huge head out of paper and tied this onto the body. A funny paper mask would be purchased from Woolworths, with Dad's oldest gardening hat placed on the guy's head. Our guy then had a place of honour in an armchair until 5 November.

A large box of assorted fireworks was bought from Woolworths, along with several packets of sparklers. My dad would have built a bonfire with any old junk that he couldn't use for anything else, and that would be roaring away, ready to set fire to the wooden clothes pole, Dad's shed and the trellis fencing if he wasn't careful. Catherine wheels were nailed to the fence and rockets were placed in glass milk or lemonade bottles with a bucket of water on standby in case the flames or fireworks escaped. Dad was in sole charge of the proceedings, with Mum screaming at him to be careful. The curly Jumping Jacks always chased him up the garden path and something was usually burnt. He put paraffin on the bonfire if the weather was damp, which was very silly and dangerous; this resulted in Mum calling him a stupid bloomer, or words to that effect.

We all sang out loud, 'Guy, guy guy, hit him in the eye. Stick him up the lamppost and there let him die.' We also sang the traditional 'Remember, remember the fifth of November, gunpowder, treason and plot. I see no reason why gunpowder treason should ever be forgot.' Our poor old guy would be sat on a box in the middle of the fire whilst we sang to him, until the flames leapt up to his head and we all shouted out 'burn, guy, burn' until he was gone for ever.

We watched the fireworks with plenty of oohs, a few aahhs and plenty of screams when the bangers went off. The sparklers were lit and waved about, and then we all went indoors for something warm to eat. This was usually a bowl of steaming hot Heinz tomato soup and crusty bread, followed by a large jacket potato cooked in the oven so the skin was lovely and crispy. This would be smothered in thick butter, salt and pepper; I loved the skin best, so every scrap would be eaten. Mum sometimes fried some sausages until the skins were almost black – just as I liked them – and we might have had a few baked beans too.

The next morning, the air would still be a bit smoky from the previous evening. The remains of the bonfire would be spread over the garden and Dad then had to collect the many spent fireworks and sparklers scattered over the grass. The only 5 November that we didn't celebrate was in 1956, because my lovely old Gran died on that day.

—

We had a small bonfire with a guy, plus some sparklers.

Tony Thomas

I remember making a guy for our bonfire and having sparklers. We always had mugs of hot soup in the garden.

Margaret Thomas, née Gilkerson

I didn't like Firework Night. We always had a bonfire in the garden and the neighbours all came round, but I stayed indoors.

Jean Palmer, née Organ

It was sparklers, a bonfire and the making of the guy. Catherine wheels, Jumping Jacks, rockets placed in a milk bottle. There were no fireworks allowed on a Sunday.

Diane Williams, née LeMettey

We always had a firework display in the back garden on 5 November. There was no bonfire or bangers, only Catherine wheels, Roman candles and a few rockets. It was all over in half an hour.

Ken Matthews

I remember making the Guy Fawkes and burning it on the big open fire in the garden. We roasted chestnuts and had family and friends over to watch the firework display. There were sparklers for all the children.

Doreen Matthews, née Linsdale

HAPPY BIRTHDAY

At the end of November I celebrated my birthday with a tea party. We usually held this event in the front room. With just the dining table and chairs in the room and canvas on the floor it was a bit chilly, especially as my friends and I would be in our party frocks, so a coal fire was lit for the afternoon. We would always dress up for the occasion, and these outfits could be worn for friends' birthday parties and Christmas celebrations too. There would be about ten special friends invited to the party, with the invitations given out at school. It was always on my actual birthday; whether or not it was a school day didn't matter. I remember coming home from school between the ages of 4 and 7 and Mum hoisting me up onto the wooden draining board for a quick wash of my face, hands and knees, which were always grubby in those days. Then my prettiest dress would be put on, with matching ribbons in my hair.

As my birthday was so close to Christmas, my parents only gave me a small gift, such as a book or a tin of paints. One year I asked for an encyclopaedia, and the red Collins New Age version still sits proudly on my shelf. In the '50s we were grateful for any present we received, and I think we appreciated them more than children do today with their mountains of possessions.

In the front room, a table was laid with a crisp white tablecloth, paper plates and cups of orange squash, lemonade or Tizer. There were dainty sandwiches with grated cheese, Shippams fish paste and egg and cress, a bowl of Smith's crisps and a plate of tiny sausage rolls. One red and one green jelly would be wobbling in bowls, with another bowl containing pink blancmange. Plates of iced biscuits and tiny iced gems – which I hated – were placed alongside Cadbury's chocolate fingers and strawberry wafers (which I loved). In the centre of the table stood the round iced birthday cake complete with candles and the words 'Happy Birthday Valerie', plus my age that year.

My friends all arrived with cards and little gifts of books, colouring pencils, games and jigsaw puzzles. To warm us up we might play a few games before tea. We would always play 'Oranges and Lemons', where two girls, one playing the role of oranges and the other as lemons, formed an arch and the rest filed through singing.

Oranges and lemons, say the bells of St Clement's.
'You owe me five farthings,' say the bells of St Martins.
'When will you pay me?' say the bells of Old Bailey.
'When I grow rich,' say the bells of Shoreditch.
'When will that be?' say the bells of Stepney.
'I do not know,' says the great bell of Bow.
Here comes a candle to light you to bed.
Here comes a chopper to chop off your head.
Chop chop, chop chop, the last man's dead.

Then the girl who came last would choose to go behind oranges or lemons and at the end, a tug of war was formed.

We would have worked up an appetite after a few games and were ready for tea; the candles would then be lit for everyone to sing 'Happy Birthday' with the lights out. Mum would have a pass the parcel made up with newspaper and a small gift in the middle for the winner for us to play afterwards.

Mum played a tune on the piano for musical chairs and statues, giving out prizes of small bars of chocolate or maybe packets of mixed fruit flavoured Spangles or Rowntree's Fruit Gums. There was also a game where everyone sat on a chair and one girl had a scarf tied round her eyes and was spun around. She then had to find a lap to sit on and say 'Ducky, ducky', to which the other girl replied 'Quack, quack', in a strange voice. The girl on her lap then had to guess who the voice belonged to. A game I was never keen on was forfeits, where you were asked a question. If you were wrong, you had to pay a forfeit by doing whatever the questioner asked of you. This might be singing a song, doing a dance or if boys were present, you might have to kiss them. We didn't play this at my party, that's for sure.

The party usually lasted around two hours, and when the mums and dads came to collect their children, each child was given a bag with a balloon, a packet of sweets and a slice of cake wrapped in a serviette. Some mothers went a bit silly with the take-home gifts and I remember receiving a silver locket at one party. There were several parties in those days as we were the baby boomer generation with classes of forty-six children and more. It could become rather expensive to attend every party, so some had to be refused.

—

Gran used to take me to the pictures either at the Tivoli, the Shaftesbury or the Victoria cinema; now all of these have long gone in Portsmouth.

Tony Thomas

I usually had a party with a small gift. We played pass the parcel, and statues, and ate jelly and fruit.

Margaret Thomas, née Gilkerson

My birthday was in the school holidays, but we didn't have parties as they do now. Mum and Dad always tried to make it special though. Dad sometimes borrowed a car from a mate and took us out for the day. Or we would get the bus and take a picnic into the countryside.

Jean Palmer, née Organ

There was always pass the parcel, musical chairs and hunt the thimble. We also had a clay pipe with bubbles to blow.

Diane Williams, née LeMettey

We always had a big birthday party with friends and family. I had lots of presents from everyone. I remember eating jelly, blancmange and a birthday cake with candles. We played several games too.

Doreen Matthews, née Linsdale

CHRISTMAS AND NEW YEAR

My mother was not a keen baker, so everything to eat for Christmas was bought, not created in our kitchen. I think Mum saved a few pounds during the year with the local shop and butcher, paying a few shillings each week into their Christmas clubs to help with the Christmas budget. The Co-operative 'divi' was paid out before Christmas, so that would have paid for a few gifts.

There was usually a shopping trip in December to the large Co-op in Fratton Road, so I could visit Father Christmas. It seemed really exciting then, as all us children were seated in a closed-in sleigh which seemed to be moving forward. When it stopped we had arrived at Father Christmas' grotto, where there were elves and fairies and lots of snow and music playing 'Jingle Bells'. We all believed we were in Lapland seeing the real Father Christmas.

I saved some of my pocket money that I received from various relations over the year to buy gifts for everyone. This meant many trips to Woolworths in North End, where they had several things that I could afford. A small plastic kitchen gadget for the aunts would be a few shillings, plus a hanky and a single cigar out of a packet of five for the uncles. I bought a bag of coloured bath salts and some jars and ribbon to make gifts for the older relations, or a few bath cubes and a bar of soap.

Dad and Mum usually gave me extra cash towards presents for each other. For my friends it would be a pretty lace hanky, a book or pencils for school. One birthday I received a craft set to make plastic brooches with lots of different coloured plastic beads to stick in with glue. This solved the problem of what to get for my friends; they all received one that year.

Most evenings before Christmas, the doorbell would be in constant use, and a few rosy-cheeked children would stand outside, singing a few words to a famous carol. As far as Mum was concerned, they would have to know at least the first verse before she parted with a few precious pennies.

I enjoyed spending a few evenings making cards and calendars for various relations, so the dining table would be covered in newspaper with coloured glitter and cotton wool scattered all over it. Mum sometimes made a snowman out of papier-mâché, which was hollow inside to fill with tiny gifts for our Christmas party. We covered the outside with cotton wool and made a hat out of cardboard painted black. My mother also used to buy a few joke gifts like Senna pods, hair nets and things she had bought in a joke shop called 'U Need Us' in Arundel Street, Portsmouth. These items were usually things like toy false teeth and dog poo, and she put these together with cheap jewellery and plastic toys into balls of cotton wool throwing these at everyone at the family party. We also made a few decorations for the tree out of pieces of foil, cotton wool and glitter and a new dress for the old fairy out of a pretty doily. I always had a large packet of gummed coloured strips to make into paper chains to go round the room. We rolled newspaper tightly together and formed it into a circle, then covered it with green and red crêpe paper. It would then be covered with holly and tinsel and decorated with glass balls before we hung it on the front door as a wreath.

Our Christmas decorations went up about a week before Christmas and we kept last year's collection in a box in the cupboard in the hallway. These were mainly made of paper, so had to be carefully packed away after the festivities were over as my parents couldn't afford new ones each year. There were coloured paper garlands to stretch across the room, with large paper bells and balls to hang from the ceiling. My paper chains were looped around the walls, with some red and green crêpe paper from a roll twisted together and placed on another wall. My father loved Christmas and was never satisfied until the place resembled Santa's grotto, with tinsel everywhere. Silver and red lametta was hung over the garlands, and ribbed silver and red foil was twisted and hung in each corner until the ceiling was completely covered. I remember that Dad had some flags left over from the Coronation and these were always put up in the passage with a lot of protesting from Mum. Dad would be standing precariously on the stepladder, leaning too far over while putting up the decorations, with my mother screaming and swearing at him to be careful. His mouth would be full of drawing pins, so if he fell we would have had a real emergency on our hands.

On the Friday before Christmas, Mum and I always met Dad from work at the Portsmouth Dockyard in the afternoon. On the way there we passed the Brickwoods brewery, with its pungent smell of hops and yeast that used to make me a bit queasy. My father would be standing at Unicorn Gate, looking very red-faced and merry, as he would have been to the pub with his mates for a Christmas drink. As we approached, he would do a little tap dance with his arms open wide to meet our embrace. He would greet us, saying something like 'Hello, my little darlings'. Up close he smelt of beer and cigarettes that were still clinging to his clothes from the pub. We would all then make our way to Charlotte Street market, which was just off Commercial Road.

By this time in late December, it would be dark, damp and rather cold, so all the market stalls would have coloured lights festooned around their awnings. The fruit and veg were full of colour and looking really fresh: large Spanish oranges, Cox's apples and ripe pears piled high. There were all kinds of nuts: walnuts, Brazils, hazelnuts, almonds and peanuts in their shells, plus a few large, hairy coconuts. The smells were appetising and there was always a strong smell of celery at Christmas too. A large white lorry was parked at one end of the market selling meat, and the stallholder had a large supply of chickens and turkey for Christmas Day. Turkey was rather expensive at the beginning of 1950s, so we had a large capon chicken instead. Mum would have ordered this from John the butcher, and paid for it from her Christmas club money.

I remember that at the market, there was always the sound of carols being sung by the Salvation Army, and my dad would have joined in the singing for a while. A man was selling hot chestnuts which Mum couldn't resist, so we shared a bag, peeling the hot shell and revealing the sweet nut inside. Mum always said on the run up to Christmas, 'Roll on Christmas and lets have some nuts.' We always sang this rhyme too:

Christmas is coming the goose is getting fat,
Please do put a penny in the old man's hat.
If you haven't got a penny, a half penny will do.
If you haven't got a half penny, then God bless you.

Some stalls sold gifts and toys, and I always loved to have a doll in my stocking every year. I was never disappointed, so I expect Mum and Dad made a trip to the market without me before Christmas. Mum bought a few of each of the fruits and some vegetables, tomatoes and celery plus a large packet of sticky dates with the wooden fork inside. Mum loved nuts, so bought a selection of the shelled variety, plus a large coconut to share. The last stop would be to buy a real Christmas tree, and I loved the scent of the fresh pine needles. The market stallholders all called out their wares to attract the customers to buy from them: 'Luverly ripe apples, missus, have a couple of coconuts for a bob. Come on, I've only got a few left. Once they're gone, missus, they're gone.'

Sadly the old Charlotte Street Market has since moved into the Commercial Road shopping precinct, and it has lost its old world charm and magic for me.

When we arrived home later that day, Dad put the tree in a bucket of earth from the garden, which Mum had covered with green crepe paper and a red bow. After Dad put the lights on – different shaped bulbs with Father Christmas heads and snowmen on – it was my job to decorate the tree. There were coloured glass balls, some which were covered in glitter, and glass birds with brightly coloured feathered tails, which clipped onto the branches. We had a few plastic icicles and snowflakes, and several handmade decorations. I had one decoration that had to be in the centre of the tree. It was a plastic Father Christmas in a sleigh, and I still have it now. A few strands of lametta were scattered over the tree and cotton wool balls were stuck on the ends, like snow. The old fairy was straightened out and stuck on the top branch. The lights in the living room were switched off and the tree lights switched on and – if all the bulbs worked – the room was ablaze with pretty colours. It looked really Christmassy, especially with the coal fire roaring away in the grate.

On Christmas Eve, Mum and Dad used to go over to the Pelham pub in Chichester Road in the early part of the evening, leaving me with Emily. I spent my time wrapping the gifts I had bought for everyone and placing them under the tree. When Mum and Dad came home smelling beery and looking merry, I was bathed and put into a new pair of cosy pink winceyette pyjamas, ready for bed. Dad put a glass of Harvey's Bristol Cream sherry and a mince pie out for Father Christmas, along with a carrot for Rudolph. I was assured by my grandfather that the coal fire would be out before Father Christmas tumbled down our chimney, although how he would have squeezed down our tiny chimney is anyone's guess. I had a clean white pillow slip to hang on the end of my bed in the hope that it might be filled with toys in the night. We always had a coal fire alight in the large bedroom on Christmas Eve, and I remember lying awake in my large cot bed, watching the reflection of the flames dart across the ceiling. I tried everything to stay awake to see the great man enter the room with his sack. The excitement most small children feel on Christmas Eve will always be remembered and no other emotion can match it. I even tried sleeping with my head facing the other end of my bed so I could catch him, but I never did. Somehow I would fall asleep, and when I woke in the early hours of the morning my feet would move to the bottom and feel the crackling of the parcels at my feet. I would then call out to my parents. 'He's been, he's been and filled my sack.'

Mum and Dad slept in the same room as me and mumbled 'that's lovely, darling' with a fake surprised look on their faces. My mum can't have been asleep long, as she and Emily used to stay up and prepare all the vegetables for the next day. They put the chicken or turkey into the oven overnight, so there was a delicious smell of cooked meat when we woke up on Christmas morning. Mum always boiled a gammon in a saucepan and cooked a piece of pork with crispy crackling to serve cold over the Christmas period.

When I was very young, all the presents from family were put into my pillow slip. There was usually a doll from Emily, doll's clothes made by an aunt, *Bunty*, *Beano* or *Dandy* annuals, boxed games and things like a post office set or a bus conductor set. Dad made some of my toys in the early part of the 1950s. I had a wooden oven, dresser and table and chairs, plus a blackboard and easel. One year I had a beautiful Pedigree pram in navy blue from Mum and Dad. My grandparents bought the pram accessories and a rattle that stretched across the hood, just like a real baby would have. Another year I had a red plastic telephone exchange with wires and plugs to pretend to put people through to each other, which I found a lot of fun. I also had metal toy like a till, but it did sums by pressing in the numbers and either adding, subtracting, multiplying or dividing; like a calculator. Another toy I played with a lot was a large blue wooden bagatelle, which was like a pin machine with silver balls that you shot round the board, trying to get the highest score.

Emily always went to her family for Christmas Day and Boxing Day, and we used to have the Christmas meal at lunchtime with just my parents and grandparents.

After eating our lovely Christmas meal – followed by a small slice of Christmas pudding with hot custard – Mum and Dad washed up and had a little snooze. I played with all my new toys and read my books with just the radio for company. By late afternoon, the relations started to arrive, if the party was to be in our house: Iris and Bob, Uncle Harold and Auntie May and their son Harold, who was on his own until he married Julie later in the 1950s. Joyce, Roy and Diane arrived much later, as the pub would have been open for just a few hours on Christmas Day.

The men in the family went over to the Pelham pub to buy a crate of beer, some lemonade and maybe a few sweet Babychams (as I was allowed one of those as I got older). Dad's wine cabinet that he made would usually contain a bottle of Teacher's whisky, Harvey's Bristol Cream Sherry and maybe a bottle of Stone's Ginger Wine. There wouldn't be wine as the family didn't drink it. The ladies congregated in our small kitchen, cooking potatoes for mashing and slicing cold meats and salads.

The trestle table used for decorating was brought in and added to the dining table, with a large cotton sheet on top as a tablecloth. Alongside the dining chairs were placed long pieces of wood and cushions for extra seating, as there were usually twelve of us round the table with only six chairs. All the food was placed along the table; as well as the cold meat, salad and hot potatoes, there were pickles, beetroot and a large vase with celery in it. The iced Christmas cake took centre stage and there was a bowl of nuts in their shells, with a pair of brass nutcrackers in the shape of a nude lady's legs. There were a few mince pies and sausage rolls and a plate of thinly sliced bread and butter, plus a bowl of fruit.

Jacobs cream crackers were on a board, with a large wedge of Cheddar cheese and one of Gorgonzola. Somebody might bring some chocolates and there was sometimes a tin of Sharpe's toffees and a box of Turkish Delight to share.

There was usually a Christmas cracker to pull with a hat to wear (one each), but one year we had a huge cracker hanging above the table that everyone had to have a tug of war to pull, with all the gifts falling onto the table. After we had eaten, someone would play Father Christmas, giving out the presents to everyone. Then Mum would either throw her snowballs around or open up the snowman she made; whichever she was using that year. The table would then be dismantled and put away to make space for fun and games. When we were very young, Diane and I were both put to sleep in my parents' double bed and the party then went on into the early hours of the morning. Sometimes the adults eventually slept where they could until the morning, and then we had another party somewhere else on Boxing Day. Mum and Dad would sleep on armchairs, as we had their bed, and one of the relations slept in the bath with a pile of blankets.

When Diane and I were old enough, we were allowed to join in the fun too. On the door to the living room was a dartboard, and the men enjoyed a game while the ladies washed up in the kitchen. One day the younger males got a bit silly and one put a balloon on his head, while another threw darts to burst it. My aunt soon put a stop to that and calmed them down. Mum and Dad always entertained the family by dressing up and singing various songs. The men sang a few rude songs that Diane and I couldn't understand: we were young and innocent in those days. We all had to sing a song, even if our voices weren't very good. Any comical song that was on the radio was always a favourite, of course. Auntie Joyce used to sing 'On the Good Ship Lollipop' in a little girl's voice. My song was 'Daisy, Daisy'.

Young Harold always brought one of his piano accordions with him; he had a lovely pearl white one and another in ruby red and he could play any tune on them. So all the family joined in with a sing-song of all the favourite songs they knew. Uncle Bob entertained Diane and me by blowing smoke rings, and turning the cigarette inside his lips and doing various tricks with matchsticks and cards.

The aim of our Christmas parties was that we were all having fun in each other's company, and everyone was included and not left on their own at Christmas. We also had parties in other houses. I remember that Auntie May had one in Pink Road. Diane and I were quite young and we were told that Father Christmas was coming to the house that evening. When we looked out of the window, there seemed to be snow falling outside (one of the adults was actually throwing cotton wool balls down from the bedroom window). When Father Christmas arrived with bells jingling, he gave out presents to everyone. Then Diane announced that he had her grandfather's shoes on.

There was also a party in the Shanty one year in the late '50s, and Uncle Harold had just bought a Grundig tape recorder. We had great fun singing our party pieces into the microphone and then playing it back. I sang 'Tom Dooley', which was in the charts that year.

Diane and I always had a children's Christmas party and a pantomime to go to, as the dockyard and the Buffaloes put these on for the children of their members. The parties were fun, with loads of food (jelly and cake), games,

Punch and Judy and of course a visit from Father Christmas and a gift. My favourite gift was a large thick book of nursery rhymes called *Tales of Mother Goose*. The pantomime would have been staged at the Kings Theatre in Southsea.

The Kings Theatre was built in 1907 and used to show films in the afternoons in the 1920s and '30s. The Kings has always been a great theatre showing plays, ballet, shows and, of course, pantomime. My grandmother, May Macklin, worked as a dresser there in the '20s or '30s and also opened her house to several famous names, who lodged with the family.

Boxing Day was also celebrated with a family party in another house, sometimes in the upstairs function room at Joyce and Roy's pub, but after that most people returned to work. We spent the rest of the week using up the cold turkey or chicken, ham and pork in various ways until it was all eaten. Although we didn't have a refrigerator, the meat stayed fresh as the house was very cold without central heating.

Our family didn't celebrate New Year at all and there wasn't any time off then. Sometimes, Mum, Dad and I stayed up and watched the BBC ring in the New Year with Andy Stewart in *The White Heather Club*. He sang all the Scottish songs, including 'Auld Lang Syne' and the comedy song 'Donald, Where's Your Troosers?' Mum and Dad toasted the New Year with a small whisky and we used up the sweets, nuts and special biscuits during the evening. Dad usually had to go outside before midnight and come back in holding a piece of coal. He had dark hair and was therefore classed as a First Footer. This is an old tradition to bring luck and fortune into the house at New Year. Some people bring a coin, salt, whisky or bread. My best friend Margaret and her mother were born in Scotland, so they celebrated New Year more than Christmas. In the later part of the 1950s, I joined her family in the New Year's Eve parties. These were quite riotous affairs, with everyone ending up out in the street doing the conga and forming a large circle in the road to do 'Auld Lang Syne'.

The dockyard also put on concerts and parties for the children at Christmas, so I am not sure whether it was there or the Buffaloes where I started and ended my stage career. I was very young – about 3 or 4, I think – and Dad spent ages cutting out pieces of suede and leather to make me a cowgirl outfit, complete with a fringed skirt and waistcoat. I had a Stetson hat, a holster with toy guns and a rifle, with boots on my feet. I thought that I just had to walk across the stage, but I was very nervous. Standing on the steps waiting with Dad to go on, I realised the child on the stage was singing a song. I didn't know the words to 'Annie Get Your Gun', which would have been appropriate for my costume. The only song I knew was 'Daisy, Daisy', and that wouldn't be right, I was sure of that. As I stood shaking with fear, the curtain pulled back a fraction and the face of a Poirette clown peeked out at me, hoping to cheer me up. This painted white face with red lips, funny-shaped black eyebrows and a cone-shaped hat did just the opposite. I screamed blue murder and cried hysterically, and Dad had to quickly take me away.

Dad changed me into my cosy one-piece dark brown real fur zip-up winter outfit with a hood and, with me looking like an escaped teddy bear, he took me home. It was cold and dark outside and I rode on Dad's strong shoulders through the streets of Portsmouth with hot tears still streaming down my cheeks. Dad must have been disappointed as he was always so proud of me and would have liked me to be musical like him and Mum, but he never said a word about it.

I was never to be put through that ordeal again and Mum felt that, as I was so shy, lessons in singing, dancing and piano would have been wasted on me after that. I did love to sing on my own, but didn't fancy a life on the stage. I was put off clowns for life, as well.

—

I made paper chains to add to the decorations. We had chicken for Christmas Dinner. I remember going down to the Guildhall square to see the large Christmas tree and all the lights, and the trolleybus was decorated with lights and a Santa. I was always taken to the Landport Drapery Bazaar department store to see Santa. As my dad was in the navy, we often went on board his ship HMS *Bulwark* for Christmas and a children's party. Dad had a clown's fancy dress outfit he used to wear for these occasions, and I sometimes wore it too.

Tony Thomas

Tony Thomas with his mother and father, Doris and Charles, onboard HMS *Bulwark*, Portsmouth Dockyard, Christmas 1955.

I made paper chains and helped with the Christmas cake and we put silver sixpences into the pudding. We had roast chicken, followed by trifle for Christmas Dinner. I remember every Christmas I received an *Oor Wullie* annual from my Scottish relations.

Margaret Thomas, née Gilkerson

We always had a fire lit in the front room at Christmas. Mum bought lots of fruit weeks before Christmas. It was a big family occasion and we had Christmas dinner at my nan's, who lived opposite. My Uncle Harry, Auntie Ethel and Bernie all came to join us. Mum and Auntie Ethel all helped with the cooking in the kitchen. We all listened to the queen's speech [the Christmas Message], although it was the king at the beginning of the 1950s.

Jean Palmer, née Organ

I always remember the lovely Christmas parties; it was either Uncle Bob's firm or the dockyard that held them. It was in a big hall, with lots of children and games to play. There was always a Father Christmas giving you a nice present. We went to the pantomime in the Kings Theatre in Southsea. Also the family parties with lots of singing [and] all the family playing different musical instruments: piano, drums, accordion, paper and comb, spoons and a xylophone. We played card and board games too with the family; there was Newmarket with pennies and halfpennies to bet with.

Diane Williams, née LeMettey

Generally I was given one large main toy, which was either a garage or Meccano set and four or five small items. There was always a stocking filled with an apple, banana, orange and some nuts.

Ken Matthews

They were wonderful times. On Christmas Day we would open all our presents and stockings delivered by Santa, which was our dad dressed up. There was a full roast chicken dinner and Christmas pud, made by Mum. In the evening there would be a sing-song around the piano followed by games.

Doreen Matthews, née Linsdale

During the war my dad, Fred, befriended some Canadian soldiers and used to bring them home for a meal. For several Christmases after that we received a large parcel of gifts from them.

John Organ

eight

THE END
OF AN ERA

In the summer of 1959, Emily was taken ill and admitted to hospital. When she was well enough to come out, she went to live with her sister Ethel in Mile End. Both my grandparents had died in 1956, so the house was almost empty of people compared to the beginning of the decade. Mum decided to get rid of all the lodgers and instead took in navy couples, who would have one room and share the bathroom and kitchen facilities, cooking their own meals. Portsmouth being a naval port, there was never a shortage of couples and they only stayed for a short while until they were transferred elsewhere in the country. Each couple we took in brought their young baby with them and we treated them like part of the family and babysat for them too.

Mum then decided to take a cleaning job in a pub for a few hours in the morning from 1960 onwards, to earn extra money. Cleaning wasn't her first choice of occupation – in fact she hated it – but she wasn't trained for anything other than that and entertaining.

Margaret and I were 13 years old in 1959, and the way we played and spent our leisure time slowly changed. We bought teen magazines such as *Mirabelle* and plastered our bedroom walls with posters of the latest pop stars; there was Tommy Steele, Joe Brown, Marty Wilde, Adam Faith, Billy Fury and Cliff Richard, to name but a few. My dear mum queued outside the Troxy cinema in Fratton Road, Portsmouth, for tickets for Margaret and me to see a live performance by Cliff Richard and the Shadows. We were both beside ourselves with happiness and screamed ourselves hoarse on the day. It was 27 April 1960.

In the early evenings we would often meet up and walk the length of North End shopping centre, looking in shop windows and stopping for a frothy coffee in the Cup and Saucer café. The coffee was served in a clear glass cup and saucer, which we thought was the epitome of sophistication at the time. Dad used to say that we were going 'up monkey parade'. If we were late getting home, both of our mothers would be waiting at the gate in front of our houses with arms folded and a severe look on their faces.

Our style of dress started to change when we entered our teens. Margaret and I wore very full skirts, puffed out with layers of net and foam petticoats, and a wide elasticated belt to cinch our waists in. Our thin cardigans were worn back to front, so they looked like a plain jumper from the front. For the first time I was allowed a pair of slip-on shoes without laces or buckles, and with a small Louie heel. That Whitsun, Mum bought me my first two-piece suit, or 'costume', as we called it then. It consisted of a navy blue straight skirt and box jacket, together with a white blouse and flat stretchy pumps. Margaret and I backcombed our hair and kept it in place with a very sticky hairspray. I bought a plastic spray bottle and you could get a refill of this sticky stuff in the hairdressers, or Woolworths. The only make-up I wore was a smudge of 'Outdoor Girl' lipstick. The shoes and the lipstick would be put on without my father knowing, as he would not have approved. Dad wasn't a strict man by any means and he was far too gentle to be violent, but a lecture from him was enough. He was keen that I didn't suffer from problems with my feet, so slip-on shoes and heels were out, and in his day, lipstick was for young girls of ill repute. Towards the end of the 1950s I had a cream trench coat with ankle-length white boots, and a silk headscarf tied round the neck and then at the back like the film stars did then. I really thought I was the business.

In 1961, the Christmas before I started work, my parents bought me my first LBD (little black dress). It was straight and short, with cap sleeves and a silk piece that draped down my back. I really felt grown up in that, with my black patent heeled shoes. I also had a brown and black mohair coat that tapered in at the knees, with large buttons down the front. I sometimes wore that dress to work the following year, as I didn't earn enough money to buy new clothes. Mum and Dad used to give me money for my birthdays each year to spend on clothes. I think it would have been £10, and I was able to buy a whole wardrobe for that amount.

PORTSMOUTH PARKS

In the summer months, Margaret and I would extend our evening walks to include a trip to Alexander Park, now known as the Mountbatten Centre. There were a few swings and a slide, and a large piece of equipment I think was called an ocean wave. Several children could sit or stand on it, and it swung round and from side to side. I believe it has been banned from parks now due to health and safety rules. The ground beneath the play equipment was concrete, so could lead to nasty accidents, I suppose. Alexander Park had plenty of grass to play on, and I remember there being a small hill you could climb and roll down. A little hut stood in the centre of the grass, where teenagers used to meet for a chat or a snog. There was an athletics area with stands for seating and we held our school city sports there. Sometimes we hired a tennis court and bashed about with a racquet and ball.

There were two other parks we went to in Portsmouth; College Park in Kirby Road, North End, and Victoria Park, close to the Portsmouth Guildhall. Victoria Park was one of the loveliest places to walk around in the 1950s. The flower beds were colourful and you could sit on a bench or the grass and enjoy an ice cream or a picnic lunch. There were small animals in cages – birds, hamsters and tortoises, I think. College Park had a large green for the bowls club, and was quiet and peaceful to walk around. I often took my neighbour's children there in their pram.

Portsmouth was badly bombed during the war, and there were huge craters and rubble all over the city when I was very young. Our Guildhall was almost completely destroyed when it was hit in 1941; the inside was blown apart, leaving just the outside which was just a shell. It was rebuilt and reopened by Queen Elizabeth II in June 1959.

nine

MEMORABLE EVENTS IN PORTSMOUTH'S HISTORY

Henry VIII ordered the construction of Southsea Castle to the east of Portsmouth, overlooking the sea, in 1544.

In 1642, during the Civil War, the military governor of Portsmouth supported King Charles I. Parliament sent men to besiege Portsmouth and Southsea Castle was taken. The guns of Southsea Castle were then fired towards the town of Portsmouth.

Isambard Kingdom Brunel was born in Britain Street, Portsea, in 1806.

Author Charles Dickens was born in Portsmouth at No.1 Mile End Terrace in 1812. The same house, now No.393 Old Commercial Road, Mile End, Portsmouth, has since become the Charles Dickens Birthplace Museum. His father John worked in the Admiralty pay office, based in Portsmouth Dockyard.

Until the nineteenth century, Portsmouth was made up of Old Portsmouth and Portsea. A new suburb was built, which later became known as Southsea after the castle. Portsmouth was granted city status in 1926.

The first houses in Southsea were built for skilled workers in the mineral streets, such as Silver Street and Nickel Street.

Rudyard Kipling lived in Campbell Road, Portsmouth, in the 1870s.

Arthur Conan Doyle came to live in Southsea. He wrote his first Sherlock Holmes story, *A Study in Scarlet*, whilst living in Elm Grove, Southsea.

The comedian Peter Sellers was born in Southsea in 1925.

Portsmouth Airport was built in 1930, and the Airspeed Ltd factory moved to Portsmouth from York in 1933. The Airspeed produced the Courier, and then during the Second World War they built the Envoy and the Oxford aircraft. After the war, they merged with De Havilland and were reduced to making aircraft components, closing in 1960. Portsmouth Airport was closed down in 1973 and the site is now called Anchorage Park, a residential and industrial site.

1949/50 was Portsmouth Football Club's 'Golden Jubilee' season. They were champions of England twice, in 1949 and 1950, attracting crowds of 55,385. Pompey had the advantage then because a lot of footballers had to move to Portsmouth to serve in the docks, so the team effectively had the pick of the best players. Unfortunately, their luck ran out in 1959 when they were relegated to the Second Division and in 1961, the team dropped again, ending up in the Third Division.

King George VI died on 6 February 1952. His daughter was declared Queen Elizabeth II.

When our queen was still a princess, she toured the City of Portsmouth on 20 July 1951. She opened the Nuffield Club and reopened the Connaught Drill Hall in Stanhope Road. In the evening she danced at Admiralty House. Her sister, Princess Margaret, made a visit on 26 June 1952 and a year later, on 15 June 1953, Queen Elizabeth II returned to Portsmouth to review her fleet at Spithead.

In 1953 a tattoo, a contest between different sections of the military, was held at Fratton Park football ground. At the end of the evening there was a spectacular firework display.

Food rationing ended completely on 4 July 1954 (clothes rationing had ended six years before). Rationing actually became worse immediately after the Second World War when bread and potatoes, in particular, remained rationed. Children had very few sweets because of rationing and so we must have had better teeth than the later generations.

This is some of the food that was rationed; this is for each person per week:
1oz. cheese
2oz. tea
2oz. jam
4oz. bacon or ham

Is worth of meat and 8oz. of fats, which only included 2oz. of butter.

Sweets were on a points system, which meant that children had to choose between a small tube of sweets and a tiny bar of chocolate each week.

Navy Days in Portsmouth Dockyard were usually held in August each year, and this gave everyone a chance to view the ships up close and have a great day out. Nelson's flagship, HMS *Victory*, was on display in the 1950s as it is today.

The Southsea Show on the Common, which is held each summer, was a very popular event in the 1950s. There were several marquees, with various produce on display such as prize-winning vegetables, flowers and plants. Stalls were set up selling anything from sweets and homemade cakes to gadgets. In the showground they held dog shows and gave prizes for the best animals. There used to be a Floral Queen competition. When the judges chose the queen and her attendants, they would all sit on their thrones for everyone to admire.

Portsmouth Guildhall was almost destroyed by bombs during the Second World War. The inside of the building was gutted, leaving just a shell. In 1959, the place was reconstructed and Queen Elizabeth II came to Portsmouth to reopen it.

The hovercraft was developed in 1959, and now operates close to Clarence Pier. This delivers passengers to Ryde, on the Isle of Wight. Travellers have a choice between a short journey on the hovercraft, or a more leisurely cruise by ferry.

The nickname Pompey is thought to have derived from the shipping industry: ships entering Portsmouth harbour would enter 'Pom.P' in their logbooks, in reference to Portsmouth Point.

Also from The History Press

BACK TO
SCHOOL

Find these titles and more at
www.thehistorypress.co.uk